S0-BZZ-668

Library of Congress

Nation-Building

RESOURCE BOOK

A B C • C L I O *Schools*

NHD
NATIONAL
HISTORY DAY

ABC-CLIO

PROJECT EDITOR

Holly Heinzer, *Project Editor*

EDITORIAL

Lynn Jurgensen, *Managing Editor*

David Tipton, *Managing Editor*

Kirk Werner, *Managing Editor*

Liza Hickey, *Editor*

Pat Carlin, *Senior Editor*

Elisabeth McCaffery, *Writer/Editor*

Allen Raichelle, *Senior Editor*

Tim O'Donnell, *Consulting Editor*

Melissa Stallings, *Consulting Editor*

MEDIA ACQUISITIONS

Caroline Price, *Manager, Media Resources*

PRODUCTION EDITOR

Vicki Moran, *Senior Production Editor*

National History Day, Inc.

Ann Claunch, *Director of Curriculum*

DESIGNERS

The Winter Group

Library of Congress Cataloging-in-Publication Data
Nation-building : resource book.
    p. cm. -- (Triumph & tragedy in history)
  Includes bibliographical references and index.
  ISBN 1-59884-013-4 (workbook : alk. paper)
  1. Nation-building--Study and teaching--Activity programs.
I. Series.
JZ6300.N383 2006
327.1'1--dc22

2006014911

COVER PHOTO: U.S. Marine Lieutenant Mark Murphy of Indianapolis, Indiana squats among refugees at a feeding center in northern Mogadishu. Twenty tons of food supplies were escorted by the U.S. Marines, first time since they started Operation Restore Hope.
Photo: Reuters/Corbis

National Archives

Contents

National Archives

About the Development Team

ABC-CLIO AND NATIONAL HISTORY DAY are proud to partner together to bring you the *Triumph & Tragedy* series. We are grateful to the team that developed the series, especially Cynthia Watson, Chris Mullin, and Brett Piersma who wrote the scholarly context and classroom activities to engage students in the process of historical inquiry. In addition, we want to thank the staff members from both organizations who provided background content and resources. A special thank you to Holly Heinzer, Caroline Price, and Vicki Moran who spent countless hours in leading the team through the development process.

CYNTHIA WATSON
NATIONAL WAR COLLEGE
Cynthia Watson grew up in a U.S. Agency for International Development family, completing two tours in Colombia and one in Thailand. She earned her M.A. in Economic History/Latin American Studies from the London School of Economics and a Ph.D. from Notre Dame University in Government & International Studies. Between 1997 and 2002 she was Associate Dean at the National War College and taught a course on strategy designed to demonstrate the link between U.S. policies and the conditions that Americans encounter at home and abroad. She has written on a variety of topics, including political violence, nuclear and conventional arms development, and civil-military relationships. Most recently, she has studied the struggle between China and Taiwan in their attempts to gain access to South America and nation-building efforts in Colombia. Dr. Watson is a member of the International Institute for Strategic Studies and a fellow of the Inter-University Seminar on Armed Forces and Society, and she serves on the editorial board of *Third World Quarterly.* She has appeared on radio and television, speaking on national security issues. Certified as native-fluent, Dr. Watson also works with Recording for the Blind and Dyslexic, making recordings for disabled Spanish speakers.

The statements, opinions, and conclusions written by Dr. Watson in this book are those of Dr. Watson. They do not necessarily represent opinions of the National War College nor do they constitute endorsement by the National War College.

CHRIS MULLIN
SANTA YNEZ VALLEY UNION HIGH SCHOOL
Chris Mullin graduated from the University of California at Berkeley with a degree in Classical Greek and Latin and received his Masters in Education from the University of California at Santa Barbara. Chris teaches Latin, AP European History, and AP United States History in the beautiful Santa Ynez Valley, California at Santa Ynez Valley Union High School. Chris has been a fellow of the Teachers Network Leadership Institute, Facilitator for the California History-Social Science Project, and has developed numerous history-related classroom activities that he has presented at state and national conferences. In 2003, Chris was named California Teacher of the Year for his passionate and innovative approaches to teaching history. Chris is dedicated to finding innovative ways to introduce primary source materials into the day-to-day teaching of history. He believes in challenging students and encouraging them to see history not as a series of verifiable facts, but rather as a compendium of open-ended questions. In lectures, he makes a point of revealing his own reflective process, in order to help students hone their own critical thinking skills.

BRETT PIERSMA
SANTA YNEZ VALLEY UNION HIGH SCHOOL
Brett Piersma received his B.A. in History and his Masters of Education and teaching credential at the University of California at Santa Barbara. He teaches AP European History, AP American Government, and College Preparatory World Cultures at Santa Ynez Valley Union High School in Santa Ynez, California. He has facilitated the California History-Social Sciences Project at UCSB and is a MetLife Fellow for the Teachers Network Leadership Institute. Brett has also co-written several award-winning classroom activities. His many passions in teaching include designing primary source-based lesson plans, increasing teacher voice and leadership in schools, increasing student access to rigorous curricula, and perfecting the use of technology in the classroom. Among his innovative techniques are dress-up nights for AP European History students that recreate an Enlightenment-era *salon,* complete with period music and debates on the works of Voltaire and Rousseau.

Foreword

The *Triumph & Tragedy* series explores three issues currently central to American public discourse: free speech, immigration, and nation-building. None of these topics has arisen overnight; in fact, they have been with us for centuries. This is because all three go to the heart of the American experience and our national aspirations: we are a nation of immigrants who dedicated our country to freedom and liberty, within our borders and across the world. Our treatment of our civil liberties, our new arrivals, and our responsibility to other nations defines who we are. As wars, economic downturns, and political upheavals have challenged this nation's commitment to its ideals, these issues have come to the forefront again and again. Each time, they have been put under the lens of contemporary fears and needs. Each time, they have evoked different responses.

Free speech, immigration, and nation-building have all been reinterpreted during the past century under a variety of conditions, for a variety of reasons. In many instances, the results have demonstrated the best facets of the American experiment. In others, they have revealed an unappealing, even tragic, side. These resource books detail the ways that Americans have dealt with free speech, immigration, and nation-building over the course of recent history, for better and for worse. They present pivotal "Defining Moments" that illustrate both the brightest periods in our history and its darkest episodes.

At their center, these resource books are devoted to providing each student with the raw materials to evaluate each issue on his or her own. In each resource book, the student will find a wide array of primary materials: laws, poems, quotations, cartoons, speeches, editorials, and images. To help students interpret these historical documents and give them a solid grounding in the topic, secondary essays, glossaries, and background material are provided as well. This material, too, has been drawn from a great variety of sources: experts in diverse fields including education, political science, history, and literature.

Together, these primary and secondary sources form the building blocks for sets of classroom activities. These activities are designed to encourage students to analyze primary documents and to use their conclusions to evaluate the ways that free speech, immigration, and nation-building have been handled throughout past centuries. Students are asked to debate, to role play, and to write creatively about the historical materials. At the conclusion of the activity, the students are asked to judge the actions of the parties involved and to unravel the complexities within each issue.

Opening each resource book, you will find a series of essays designed to introduce students to each topic. The first essay is a broad issue overview. The second essay is more specific and chronological. Next, the resource books present two "Defining Moments" — landmark historical events that illustrate the nature of debate on each topic. Each Defining Moment section begins with detailed background information. Then you will find the classroom activities, with instructions and a list of materials needed to complete them. These materials, primary sources and reference pieces, follow each classroom activity section. The activities are broken down into parts, each one designed to challenge the students' assumptions and lead them to different conclusions. The last portion of the activity asks the students to assess both the Defining Moment and the issue at large.

In partnering to compile the *Triumph & Tragedy* series of resource books, ABC-CLIO and National History Day, Inc. continue their commitment to challenging students with historical material that both celebrates and complicates our concept of the national heritage. By combining quality research with active learning, we hope to bring the excitement of lively history and participatory civics to your classroom.

BECKY SNYDER
President, Schools Publisher
ABC-CLIO

CATHY GORN
Executive Director
National History Day

Preface

For young adults, it is simply not enough to read texts about vital issues at the heart of American citizenship. Like the generations before them, our students are going to grapple with these topics in their lifetimes. They need to prepare by turning a critical eye upon the histories of free speech, immigration, and nation-building. Their understanding of the past will help them to make sense of the present and to make informed decisions in the future. Teaching students to examine these issues as related to the theme of *Triumph & Tragedy* will provide a framework with which to push past the antiquated view of history as mere facts and dates and drill down into historical content to develop perspective and understanding.

Students sometimes learn history fast and without meaning. The discipline is vast, and the current educational climate emphasizes coverage of content over depth. Class design is often determined by time periods and approached chronologically. But without a guiding framework, students are abandoned to isolated pieces of historical information. A theme redefines how history is learned. Instead of concentrating on the whole century or a broad topic, students are invited to stop and analyze a smaller event, a part of the story, and place it in the context of the whole. Teaching with a theme ensures that students are not overwhelmed with the sheer vastness of the field but are invited to look deeply into a manageable portion of it instead.

Triumph & Tragedy provides students with a lens to read history, an organizational structure that helps them to place information in the correct context, and finally, gives them the ability to see connections over time. We invite your students to extend their study of free speech, immigration, and nation-building by engaging in active research and presentation.

A Delicate
Balance
between
Choice and
Force

Introduction

Corbis-Bettmann

Corbis/Bettmann

A Delicate Balance between Choice and Force

Author

CYNTHIA A. WATSON
NATIONAL WAR COLLEGE

Today, the issue of nation-building is as multifaceted and complex as any current public policy issue. In fact, the modern definition of nation-building as a concept tends to depend upon the views of the people discussing it. Generally, contemporary nation-building involves creating the conditions that make it possible to construct a national identity and the functioning institutions by which the people of a defined geographic entity can build a government under which to live. Nation-building is sometimes instituted from within a country and the nation is built from the inside out. But nation-building may involve outside intervention by another nation or body for a variety of reasons: peacekeeping, preemption, humanitarian relief, institution-building, conflict avoidance, liberation, or revenge. To a great extent, nation-building is limited only by the goals of the state advocating it. The difference in perspectives is not limited to political views within the United States. European visions of nation-building are generally more interventionist and less military-based than those of the United States.

As with many complex political concepts, the term "nation-building" remains flexible and even controversial. The notion does not enjoy universal acceptance. Some critics reject some or all of the activities that define it above. Disagreement about nation-building extends to the most basic questions about its form and function. For example, it is not clear if successful and legitimate nation-building must take place wholly within a nation. It is also unclear whether or not nation-building *can* take place entirely from within. If a nation can institutionalize all of the changes to its society that are basic to nation-building, it may be able to sustain them. A program that can not stay the course will fail.

At the same time, it is debatable whether or not nation-building can be imposed on a nation by an external power. Much of the evidence from the 20th century indicates that it is virtually impossible for nation-building to be imposed on a people by outsiders. The United States has attempted to bring governmental change to Haiti, Somalia, Bosnia, Japan, Germany, Afghanistan, Iraq, Colombia, and the Philippines, and it is arguable that only in Japan and Germany has the effort been successful.

Another key question confronts any nation that has decided to go forward with a nation-building effort: *Should civil authorities or the military carry it out?* In the case of the United States, this is a significant problem. The American military is often reluctant to get involved in nation-building situations. The armed forces have always prided themselves on being involved in external issues that guarantee the defense of the United States. Defense has most often been envisioned as the destruction of an opponent or the defeat of a threat from outside the country. This is a fairly straightforward mission, with clear objectives and measures of success. Nation-building, rather, is complex and nuanced, marked by stops and starts. Given the differences between their traditional mission and the demands of nation-building, the military's opposition to involvement in nation-building should be obvious. Traditionally, the military has conceived of nation-building as a civilian responsibility. The U.S. armed forces have only taken on police functions in the most extreme national emergencies. But, on the other hand, the military is seen as more efficient, more effective, and better funded for nation-building activities than most civil authorities.

A Delicate Balance between Choice and Force, cont.

No doubt, some of the confusion about who should perform nation-building arises from disagreement about the types of situations that require nation-building responses. Disasters, natural and man-made, usually prompt outside powers to attempt to restructure other nations: famines, floods, earthquakes, wars, civil uprisings, and genocide are all on the list of motivating factors. "Peacekeeping operations" indicate that an armed conflict is in the process of ending and that a neutral force, usually foreign, is providing a buffer acceptable to all sides in the conflict. "Humanitarian operations" are generally thought of as the least invasive type of activity: the goal being to respond to an emergency often caused by a physical disaster. But even these types of missions can evolve into military engagements, through what is known as "mission creep." A perfect example of this progression is the United States' mission to provide food to Somalia in late 1992. This began as a humanitarian operation because people were starving after Somali warlords restricted the distribution of food by outside groups. The humanitarian work, however, had evolved by 1993 into a peacekeeping mission. Confusion about the nature of nation-building can arise when politicians and other policymakers use descriptive terms interchangeably. Add to this the fact that, in practice, nation-building can be many things at once: it may involve military action, humanitarian non-governmental operations, and diplomatic activities.

Although nation-building lays out a theoretical goal, the motivations behind nation-building efforts are often called into question. Nation-building has long been the focus of concerns about the true nature of any state's intentions when it violates the sovereignty of another state and then creates a new form of government for it. An example of this sort of skepticism arose at the end of World War II. The vast destruction of Western Europe called for a massive rebuilding effort. When the U.S. financed the European reconstruction under the Marshall Plan, many critics said that this was really an attempt to bring European democracies into the U.S. orbit through economic assistance, rather than allowing those states to pursue their own courses of development. More recently, critics have charged that U.S. intervention in Iraq was really about exploiting petroleum and the Iraqi economy — and had little to do with concern for the Iraqi people.

Misunderstandings and dissent are both very common when it comes to an issue as complex and controversial as nation-building. Very often, those on the home front of the builder nations become frustrated by the expenditure of resources or perceived lack of progress. In America, popular opposition to one nation-building effort — Vietnam — remains a red flag about the political, military, and cultural quagmire that can result from such projects. Many Americans still recall the street protests that accompanied the deployment of 500,000 U.S. troops in Southeast Asia in the late 1960s and early 1970s. Presidents since Lyndon Johnson and Richard Nixon have been leery of actions overseas for fear of the "body bag" phenomenon: the daily casualty counts on news programs that were so important to raising public doubts about the wisdom of nation-building in Vietnam. President Ronald Reagan withdrew U.S. marines from Lebanon in the 1980s after attacks on U.S.

A Delicate Balance between Choice and Force, cont.

forces there, as did President Bill Clinton from Somalia a decade later. Many analysts fear that this image of U.S. forces being thwarted in their nation-building efforts affects the popular support for presidents, while others say that U.S. resolve is so strong that in most cases that the "body bag" issue is non-existent. The people's response to their country's attempts to nation-build can be unpredictable and have unanticipated results.

Timing is very much at issue in nation-building as well: *When should it begin?* This is a crucial question because nation-building efforts often grow out of wars or civil conflicts: when a society is breaking down, outside powers must sometimes intervene to prevent more bloodshed or to keep the violence from escalating. Some observers believe that nation-building cannot start until all hostilities come to a complete halt, while others believe that peace operations may most importantly mean peace*making*. But the dangers and difficulties of nation-building are greatly multiplied during periods of open hostilities. Some observers believe that nation-building should be one part of a broader period called "peace maintenance operations." This is one of the harder concepts upon which the international community must find agreement.

If no one agrees on when a nation-building project should get underway, then it should come as no surprise that there is little consensus on how success should be measured and at what point the undertaking can be judged complete. If the nation-building effort lets a country choose its own path, the result could be quite different from that of a stable, traditional democracy such as France, the United States, or Britain. The temptation, however, is to "mirror image" from one society to another, thus dragging out the experience. Seasoned practitioners of nation-building express serious reservations about this problem as much as any other. In Iraq, the United States has had to fight the temptation to say that everything must be perfect before the Iraqi nation is completely rebuilt. Some observers fear that this attitude will preclude the United States from ever leaving. Nation-building is difficult precisely because there is no easily identifiable way to know that success has been achieved.

Nation-building is as complicated as any other public policy question facing any state. For each decision taken, tradeoffs are made. The perspective of what is "best" or "worst" largely lies in the eye of the beholder rather than in some objective "best" answer to a tough question. Although history is no guarantee of the future, in general, nation-building has been successful only when done from within because the challenges facing outsiders in any culture or society are so vast. Undoubtedly, however, nation-building appears one of the predominant challenges facing the world in this decade, if not this century.

The Many Faces of Nation-Building

Throughout History

Associated Press

AP/Wide World Photos

Colonial Nation-Building
Antiquity to 1919

Author

CYNTHIA A. WATSON
NATIONAL WAR COLLEGE

The concept of nation-building is neither new nor unique to the early years of the 21st century. Centuries ago, the ancient Romans and Persians spread their empires across vast areas of the world. They would probably have claimed that they were bringing civilization to the uncivilized and building strong new nations for those they conquered. Nineteenth-century British and French colonials certainly believed they too were nation-builders as they laid claim to territory in Africa and Asia and amassed great empires. U.S. settlers built a nation by conquering the North American continent over the course of two centuries. They pushed westward from the eastern seaboard until they achieved what they saw as America's "Manifest Destiny": the nation's ultimate fate to occupy the territory all the way from the east to the west coasts. All three of these groups met with varying degrees of success in their nation-building efforts. These three examples illustrate that nation-building historically focused on one people's ability to take and hold territory and maintain influence over the resident population, often by force.

Late 19th-century map showing the extent of the British Empire: the culmination of centuries of colonial nation-building by Great Britain.

Time Life Pictures/Getty Images

Structural Nation-Building
1919–1947

Modern nation-building started at the end of World War I. Several multi-ethnic empires were dissolved at the Versailles peace talks in 1918–1919. The European tradition of creating empires was giving way to a new emphasis on self-determination for the smaller nations of Europe. Statesmen at Versailles attempted to create states in which geographic boundaries would coincide with the residence of people of a single, unified ethnic or religious group. Several states in Eastern Europe were created in this way, such as Austria, Hungary, Czechoslovakia, Yugoslavia, and Turkey. This redrawing of the map of Europe was the initial round of nation-building in the 20th century. States such as Yugoslavia or Austria were envisioned as entities that would serve the needs of their people locally rather than addressing them from a distant imperial seat. Unfortunately, as the 20th century ended, the imperfections of the scheme led to the bloody disintegration of Yugoslavia. The savagery of the civil war and genocide there necessitated international intervention, which in turn led to another course of nation-building.

Perhaps the greatest triumph for American nation-building took place in the aftermath of World War II. This was the Marshall Plan, named after Secretary of State and former Army General George Catlett Marshall, who announced it in June, 1947. The Plan was one of a series of steps aimed at rebuilding a shattered Europe so thoroughly devastated by the war with Germany. The Plan granted financial assistance to the states to help rebuild institutions, buildings, and societal infrastructure. It was hoped that this money would buy time for the European governments to regain their peoples' trust and earn their patience. Contented populations would be less likely to turn to radical governments for solutions to the problems of reconstruction. During the past sixty years, critics of the Plan have argued its goals were less benign; they claim that it was the opening gambit in the Cold War, an attempt by the United States to block Soviet encroachments into western Europe. But most people still look back on the Marshall Plan with much pride in its generosity. By the early 1960s, the western European states were back on their feet. Democratic governments were in place, much of the damage was repaired, and the war was fading into memory.

Political Nation-Building
1947–1990

Library of Congress

A jeep bound for Asia c. late 1940s. With a mixture of self-interest and generosity, the Marshall Plan called for the United States to supply financial and practical support for nations rebuilding in the wake of World War II.

With the end of World War II, global thinking on nation-building moved away from attempts to create homogeneous nations toward attempts to create states for specific political goals. The Soviet Union sought to export Communism to other countries as a way of bolstering its own power. First, the Soviets tried to win allies through economic subsidies. When that failed, the Soviets did not hesitate to invade their neighbors militarily. To counter the growing influence of Moscow, the United States bolstered regimes, often nondemocratic, which allowed free markets. It was hoped that U.S. support would keep these nations out of the Soviet sphere. Essentially, the two superpowers were engaged in a global tug-of-war. Peoples and nations were pulled toward one side or the other. The game could be a ruthless one as both nations competed for the greatest worldwide influence.

This period of nation-building saw the most prolonged and tragic period for the United States to date. This was the nation's involvement in Vietnam from roughly 1954 through April 30, 1975. Vietnam had been a French colony since the 1800s. By the end of World War II, growing Vietnamese nationalism led to a desire for home rule: the nation governing itself. The United States viewed the unfolding events through the lens of the Cold War. The American government thought that the Soviet Union was behind Vietnam's attempt to create a nation of its own; the U.S. could not see Vietnamese actions as separate from assumed Communist global subversion of "democratic" regimes. The United States decided to intervene militarily.

Humanitarian Nation-Building
1990–2001

Sending hundreds of thousands of troops to fight an ill-defined war against nationalist forces proved incredibly divisive for the U.S. public. To make matters worse, U.S. forces found themselves unable to defeat an opponent of far less technological sophistication but greater endurance. The sheer length of the war, its cost in lives and resources, and the memory of the deep fissures it opened in American society have colored every nation-building attempt undertaken since.

Mobs of South Vietnamese citizens seek sanctuary within the U.S. embassy in Saigon as North Vietnamese forces approach the city, April 29, 1975. Images such as these captured the failure of U.S. nation-building efforts in Vietnam.

AP/Wide World Photos

After the Cold War wound down in the early 1990s, the great nation-builders lost their ideological goal of promoting or containing Communist expansion. Instead, the focus shifted to humanitarian assistance. The United Nations took the lead in this new era of nation-building. The international agency took its first steps in this direction in the late 1980s when it brokered a peace between Iran and Iraq, which had been at war for eight years. The U.N. success raised the possibility that there was a role for a non-ideological, supranational organization in various nation-building activities around the world. The world began to take note of the growing number of places where international intervention would help to create and sustain peaceful development.

Humanitarian Nation-Building
1990–2001, cont.

In 1992, the U.N. Secretary General, Boutros Boutros-Ghali, advocated a significant increase in several categories of developmental nation-building activities in *The Agenda for Peace Preventive Diplomacy, Peacemaking and Peacekeeping*. This optimistic document sought to throw off the dark controlling elements of the Cold War in favor of cooperation among U.N. members to encourage national self-determination, worldwide economic development, and peace among nations. Boutros-Ghali proposed that the United Nations use a combination of diplomacy and military action to secure these ends. Battle-weary after decades of struggle against the Soviets, the United States and its allies voiced significant doubts about the necessity for or efficacy of this new approach.

Several highly visible events in the 1990s forced the international community to act. The United Nations was forced to send in peace keepers to separate warring sides. It also allocated troops for immediate recovery assistance in natural disaster situations. The list of nations requiring assistance grew until it included Bangladesh, Somalia, Haiti, Rwanda, Bosnia-Herzegovina, Kosovo, and Liberia, among others. The United States was ambivalent about U.N. calls for resources. Many Americans had hoped that the end of the Cold War would seriously scale back U.S. involvement around the world. The United States had another reason for its lack of enthusiasm about participating in U.N. operations. In 1992, the United Nations sent troops to the African nation of Somalia in an effort to end a deadly civil war. The mission was unsuccessful overall. But America suffered a very public defeat when Somalis protesting the U.S. intervention shot down a Blackhawk helicopter, killing crew members and dragging the body of a U.S. Army Ranger through the streets of Mogadishu. The public outcry forced President Bill Clinton to bring U.S. troops home amidst national frustration and shock.

Somalis throw stones at a passing U.S. military truck in Mogadishu on February 24, 1993. The image of citizens turning against troops that had come to help them demonstrates the complicated nature of humanitarian nation-building.

AP/Wide World Photos

This experience did not give the United States much relish for participating in U.N. ventures. But there is also a long history at work: this nation generally stands apart from much of the rest of the world because of its tradition of not trusting supranational organizations. The United States prefers to remain in control of its troops, its funding, and its overall goals. There are also concerns that the United Nations is too bureaucratic to cope with the serious needs of a state. One spectacular failure of U.N. management may bear out American reluctance to follow agency policy. Because international cooperation does not always breed quick action, hesitation to act among U.N. nations led to genocide in Rwanda in 1994. Despite a series of warnings about the coming disaster, most of the world simply turned its back on millions of men, women, and children, leaving virtually only the Canadians to answer the cries for help. An estimated one million Rwandans were killed during the ethnic cleansing.

During the 2000 U.S. presidential campaign, candidate Governor George W. Bush voiced the concerns of the military and much of the population concerning the global nation-building commitments envisioned by the United Nations. He spoke of the nation's "comfort fatigue" at the idea that the United States had to respond to all of these situations. Bush raised the possibility that nation-building missions were sapping our national resources and interfering with our military's primary function: to protect the United States. Candidate Vice President Al Gore portrayed the nation-building enterprise more positively but urged caution by recalling the Somali experience a few years earlier.

Composite Nation-Building
2001–Present

Rwandan women walk along a path next to a mass grave holding hundreds of victims of the 1994 genocide. The U.N. failure to prevent millions of deaths hints at the limits of humanitarian efforts and has caused the United States to rethink its endorsement of U.N. priorities.

The shattering events of September 11, 2001, fundamentally altered President George W. Bush's views on the utility of conventional, 1990s-style nation-building. A new basic premise emerged: nation-building to prevent the development of brutal, terror-driven regimes seeking to destroy Western civilization. President Bush equated nation-building with democracy-building. Although there was no consensus on how this would be done or by whom, Bush reiterated that building stable democracies around the globe would be crucial for the world security into the foreseeable future. The government illustrated this new approach by arguing for the overthrow of Saddam Hussein and the need to build a Western-style, democratic nation in Iraq. In March, 2003, the United States went to war to put the ideas into practice. This was the most controversial decision since Vietnam. It is widely debated for two reasons: first, there is no agreement about whether this type of nation-building is even possible through direct intervention, and second, it is not clear that even success will be worth the cost in U.S. blood and treasure.

Current questions about nation-building center on whether or not U.S. attempts to build democratic nations will prevent the spread of international terrorism. The scope of this vision of nation-building is much broader, potentially more costly, and more interventionist than the 1990s humanitarian view. What is more, this style of nation-building may oust a country's existing government, flying directly in the face of the U.N. policy of encouraging national self-determination. The U.S. argument is that when democratic institutions are established, more inclusive societies will follow, satisfying the population and making it less likely to produce terrorists. However, it is not clear if positive outcomes will go far enough in alleviating the problems that spawn terrorism.

Little indication exists that the debate is near resolution. As the United States and, to a lesser extent, world communities have engaged in basic nation-building in Iraq and Afghanistan, other claims on world attention have arisen, such as the catastrophic Asian *tsunami* of December, 2004. There will no doubt be more stresses and distractions in the future. The world still seems inclined to engage in nation-building, as it has been for twenty years, but the United States has begun to deviate from the course set by the United Nations. Constraints within the U.S. system are making its full participation less likely as the process continues to evolve.

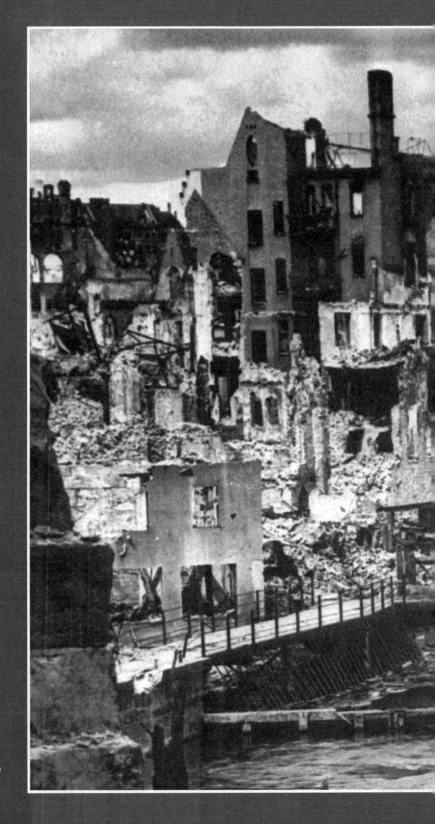

Building
Alliances,
Combating
Communism,
and Fostering
Recovery

Defining Moment

NATO Photos

National Archives

Building Alliances, Combating Communism and Fostering Recovery

The Marshall Plan, originally called the European Recovery Plan, was conceived as an effort to jump-start European reconstruction after World War II. In the early years of the Cold War, the United States was interested in containing the threat of Soviet expansion as well as in expanding its own foreign policy—and economic influence—particularly in Western Europe. World War II had left Europe in political and economic chaos. Following the surrender of Nazi Germany in the spring of 1945, the Soviet Union occupied the Eastern European territory, which its troops had taken control of during the long march to Berlin, and was determined to control its western flank. Western European nations, whose economies had been devastated by a decade of depression followed by six years of war and occupation, were ripe for political dissent. The Soviet Union was eager to take advantage of that dissent by supporting indigenous Communist movements in the West.

Library of Congress

A powerful member of the Bolshevik Party during the Russian Revolution, Joseph Stalin rose to become the successor to Vladimir Lenin as the leader of the Soviet Union. Stalin led his country through the formative years of its existence, through World War II, and finally through the early years of the Cold War. He was a defining figure of the Soviet state and of 20th-century totalitarianism. As a dictator, he carried out a ruthless series of purges in which he imprisoned and killed millions of rivals and dissidents.

By the end of the particularly difficult winter of 1946–1947, Western Europe was in serious economic distress. Food reserves in Germany were extremely low, and Communist political parties were gaining strength rapidly in France and Italy. In June 1947, U.S. Secretary of State George C. Marshall outlined a comprehensive aid package for Europe "directed not against any country or doctrine, but against hunger, poverty, desperation, and chaos." Even the Soviet Union was invited to participate, but Soviet leader Joseph Stalin declined because the terms would have forced a reduction of the Kremlin's influence in

Eastern Europe. Poland, Czechoslovakia, and Hungary also declined in response to pressure from Moscow. Despite Marshall's characterization of the recovery plan as not being directed against a particular country, clearly the intent was to limit Soviet influence in Western Europe by improving economic conditions; at the same time, however, the plan would have a powerful stimulating influence on the U.S. economy. Much of the aid would ultimately return to the United States in the form of orders for American goods.

In his speech, Marshall proposed that the nations of Europe outline a comprehensive plan for their own economic recovery—with U.S. financial support. In July, 1947, the Conference (later Committee) of European Economic Cooperation met in Paris to begin drafting a plan in response to Marshall's offer. By September, they had completed a detailed, four-year program and submitted it to Washington. Throughout the fall of 1947 and into the winter of 1948, Truman and Marshall campaigned in Washington and throughout the country for support for the measure.

A young girl holds a bouquet of hydrogen-filled balloons that carry a message of peace to communist East Europe at the spring fair in Vienna, Austria, on March 25, 1951. More than 50,000 balloons with the message "Marshall Plan 1951 Friede, Freiheit, Wohlstand" (Peace, Freedom, Welfare) were released by visitors. A postcard attached to each expressed the hope that "someday goods and products will flow freely across the countries of a united and prosperous Europe."

Associated Press

Building Alliances, Combating Communism, and Fostering Recovery, cont.

In mid-March, the Senate passed the Economic Cooperation Bill by a margin of 69 to 17, and on April 2, 1948, the House passed it 329 to 74; the following day, Truman signed it. Sixteen countries took part in the Marshall Plan. Virtually all non-Soviet bloc European nations (except Spain) received aid. West Germany became a participant when it gained self-government in 1949. By the time the plan was brought to a close in December, 1951 (six months ahead of schedule because of the Korean War), some $12 billion in grants and $1.5 billion in repayable loans had been transferred. Unlike more modern foreign aid, the Marshall Plan was aimed not at initial building in largely undeveloped economies but at rebuilding a well-developed but heavily damaged economy. It was particularly focused on such basic structural elements as the energy sector and heavy industry. It was also contingent on international cooperation among the nations receiving the aid.

The plan was a success; it greatly increased production levels in Europe and enhanced trade—not just between Europe and the United States but also among the nations of Europe. It also helped bring about economic cooperation within Europe and reduced barriers to trade. Perhaps most important to the U.S., it helped stabilize pro-Western administrations in Western European nations and greatly reduced the threat of Soviet influence. Because the Marshall Plan demonstrated the direct link between aid-supported economic development and pro-Western political stability, it soon became the model for the bulk of U.S. foreign policy throughout the Cold War. By 1949, Truman was able to propose an expanded version of the plan to benefit other, less developed regions of the world. In what became known as the Four Point Plan, President Truman proposed to extend the benefits of the Marshall Plan; relieve hunger in other, war-torn areas of the world; provide U.S. support for the United Nations; and strengthen "freedom-loving nations against the dangers of aggression."

Lesson Overview

This activity is designed to let students explore the end of World War II and the U.S. nation-building activities that grew out of it. They will need a general background in the end of the war and the position that the U.S. occupied on the international stage as a result. The focus is on the Marshall Plan (1947), the American blueprint for reconstructing post-war Europe. This activity is divided into three parts.

In Part I, the students will read quotes from the Marshall Plan and related documents and images, and discuss respective U.S. and European positions and needs.

In Part II, the students will read more of the Marshall Plan and view a series of political cartoons, trying to write captions for each as they wrestle with the visual messages.

In Part III, the students will examine the ways that the Marshall Plan was put into action, and analyze the motives of the U.S., Western Europe, and Eastern Europe, using what they have learned to uncover the beginnings of the Cold War and the nation-building wars that resulted from it.

Building Alliances, Combating Communism, and Fostering Recovery

Authors

CHRIS MULLIN
SANTA YNEZ VALLEY
UNION HIGH SCHOOL

BRETT PIERSMA
SANTA YNEZ VALLEY
UNION HIGH SCHOOL

Lesson Plan Part I
The Need for European Recovery

To prepare for this portion of the activity, the teacher should copy and post Sources 1–12 on the walls around the room. (The teacher should laminate these if possible). The teacher should also photocopy Activity Sheet 1 titled "European Need for Recovery after World War II," one for each student.

The teacher begins by explaining to students that they will be learning several of the primary factors that prompted the United States to pass the Marshall Plan. Students will do this by viewing several important primary sources ranging from quotes to images to a map. The teacher passes out one copy of Activity Sheet 1 to each student and instructs students to spend ten-to-fifteen minutes walking around the room reading and viewing documents and completing the worksheets. The Sources consist of quotes, images of devastated Europe, and a map showing the Iron Curtain and Communism. The teacher might have to describe the meaning of several of these documents depending on the academic level of the students.

The teacher debriefs the activity by posing the following questions to the class:

- According to Marshall, what was the most serious danger facing European countries after the war?
- Based on the Atlantic Charter, what type of postwar Europe did President Roosevelt and Prime Minister Churchill envision?
- To what extent did the spread of Communism into Europe pose a threat to this vision?
- Based on Source 9, how far into Europe had the Soviet's spread their influence?
- Which factor do you think contributed the greatest pressure on the United States to help Europe recover?

Activity
LESSON PLAN PART I

For this portion of the activity, students will need copies of:

ACTIVITY SHEETS
- Activity Sheet 1, p. 25

You will need copies of:

PRIMARY SOURCES
- Sources 1–12, pp. 31–42 (large enough to be read at a slight distance)

Activity Sheet 1

European Need for Recovery after World War II

The pictures, cartoons, and quotes you will view around the room depict various aspects of the condition in Europe after World War II. For each document you view, describe what you see or read in the first column. Then decide if this represents an Economic, Humanitarian, or Ideological factor in prompting America to aid in European recovery. Some documents might fall into more than one category. An example is provided for you.

Description and Basic Summary of the Source	Economic	Humanitarian	Ideological	Detailed Explanation of How
#6 Excerpt from Marshall's speech describing European need for food for next four years.		X	X	Without American aid in the form of food, many will suffer and the political situation will decay, perhaps to the point of radicals (Socialists, Communists, Nazis) taking over European countries.
# __				
# __				
# __				
# __				
# __				
# __				
# __				
# __				
# __				

Lesson Plan Part II
America's Response

In this part of the activity, students will learn about America's response to the growing needs in Europe after World War II and will analyze political cartoons that express a variety of opinions about the Plan. The teacher first makes photocopies of the last Excerpts from the Marshall Speech (Source 13, both pages), as well as each cartoon (Political Cartoons 1A–8A and 1B–8B). The teacher divides students into eight equal-sized groups and gives each group a copy of Source 13 and one of the "A" cartoons. The teacher explains to students that these cartoons have had all the captions and titles deleted, but that they all refer to the Marshall Plan. The student's task is to start by reading the Marshall Plan and discussing its implications. Then, as a group, they should analyze the cartoon and create captions. The teacher instructs students to label as many individuals or objects in their cartoon as possible and create a title for it. The teacher explains that once completed, the students' cartoons should make a political statement about the Marshall Plan.

Once students have completed their cartoons, the teacher passes out the "B" cartoons, which are the originals with captions. Some have additional explanations to aid students in their interpretation. The groups should compare their cartoon with the original by answering the following questions on a separate sheet of paper:

- What do you think the political statement of the original cartoon is?
- Why do you think the artist wanted to make that statement?
- How does your cartoon differ?
- How can political cartoons give insight and help historians interpret historical events?

The teacher debriefs this portion of the activity by having student groups show their cartoons and share their answers to the questions. The teacher fills in any gaps in students' understanding of the cartoons and discusses the cartoons with the class.

Activity
LESSON PLAN PART II

For this portion of the activity, you will need copies of:

PRIMARY SOURCES
- Source 13: Excerpt from Marshall Speech, pp. 43–44 (both pages; 8 copies)
- Cartoons 1A–8A, pp. 45–52 (8 copies)
- Cartoons 1B–8B, pp. 53–60 (8 copies)

Lesson Plan Part III
The Results of the Marshall Plan

For the final portion of the activity, students will divide into eight groups again and view pictures of Germans working at rebuilding their country as a result of the Marshall Plan. They will also view propaganda posters created by the Western Allies to encourage support for the program. The teacher will project or photocopy Images 1–6 and pose the following questions:

- Why did the United States place the logo ("For European Recovery . . . ") on each shipment?
- Interpret the "Wind mill" and "Boat" posters. What is the message? (ERP=European Recovery Program)

Next, the students stay in their groups, and the teacher explains that that they will now work with a blank map to decide how to allocate money from the United States to European countries. The teacher passes out to each group a copy of Activity Sheet 2. The teacher may want to enlarge the map for ease of use with groups and may need to provide atlases. Before writing anything on their maps, the teacher instructs students to discuss the following questions as a group:

- Based on your knowledge of World War II, which countries in Europe do you think will need the most aid? Which countries might need the second most aid, and so forth? Why?
- What is the condition in Germany after the War? Who controls East Germany?
- For what reasons did some countries not receive Marshall Plan aid?

Activity
LESSON PLAN PART III

For this portion of the activity, students will need copies of:

ACTIVITY SHEETS
- Activity Sheet 2, p. 29 (8 copies)

PRIMARY SOURCES
- Images 1–6, pp. 61–66 (8 copies)

- Image 7, p. 67 (8 copies)

Lesson Plan Part III
The Results of the Marshall Plan, cont.

Now, students should work together to label the blank map on Activity Sheet 2 with the names of each country. The teacher writes on the board in large letters "$12 billion ($12,000 million)" and explains that students' task will be to divide $12 billion of the $13.6 billion dollars that was eventually allocated under the program. The teacher explains that students should divide the money based on what they perceive to be the greatest need and should only include the following countries: Portugal, France, Belgium, Ireland, United Kingdom, Norway, Sweden, Denmark, Netherlands, West Germany, Austria, and Italy.

Once students have completed their maps, the teacher passes out a copy of Image 7 with its chart of actual money sent to each country. Student groups compare their results with the actual levels of funding and discuss the implications using the following questions:

- What do you think the consequences will be of the rejection of funding by East European states?
- Why was so much money given to France and Great Britain and considerably less to West Germany?
- Were there any nations you thought received too much or too little funding? Why?

Activity Sheet 2

Allocation of Marshall Plan Aid to European Countries

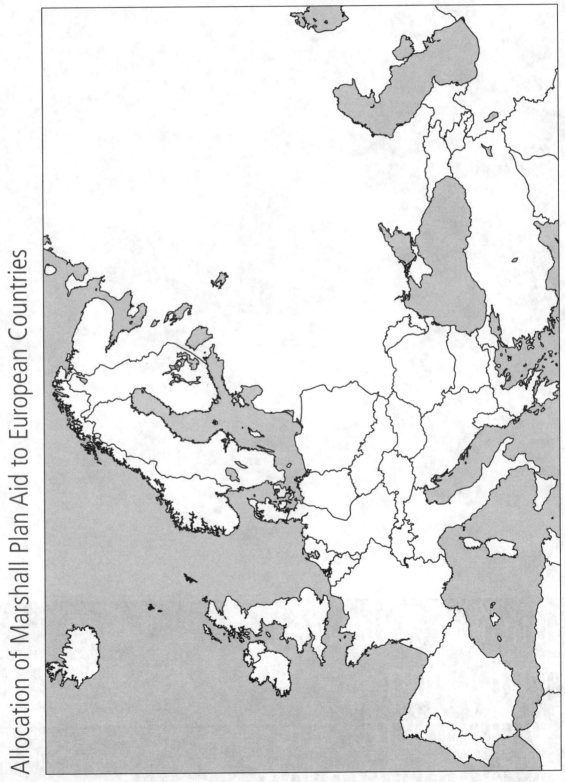

Primary Sources

Building Alliances, Combating Communism, and Fostering Recovery

Sources 1–6 are excerpts from George C. Marshall's speech at Harvard University, June 5, 1947. Sources 7 and 8 are excerpts from The Atlantic Charter agreement between President Roosevelt and Prime Minister Churchill, August, 1941. Source 9 is a map showing Europe after World War II. Source 13 contains excerpts from the second half of George C. Marshall's June 5, 1947 speech.

Source 1
Excerpt from Marshall Speech (1947)

I need not tell you gentlemen that the world situation is very serious . . .
the people of this country are distant from the troubled areas of the
earth and it is hard for them to comprehend the plight and consequent
reactions of the long-suffering peoples, and the effect of those
reactions on their governments in connection with our efforts to
promote peace in the world.

Source 2
Excerpt from Marshall Speech (1947)

In considering the requirements for the rehabilitation of Europe, the physical loss of life, the visible destruction of cities, factories, mines, and railroads was correctly estimated . . . The feverish preparation for war and the more feverish maintenance of the war effort engulfed all aspects of national economies. Machinery has fallen into disrepair or is entirely obsolete. Under the arbitrary and destructive Nazi rule, virtually every possible enterprise was geared into the German war machine. Long-standing commercial ties, private institutions, banks, insurance companies, and shipping companies disappeared, through loss of capital, absorption through nationalization, or by simple destruction.

Source 3
Excerpt from Marshall Speech (1947)

In many countries, confidence in the local currency has been severely shaken. The breakdown of the business structure of Europe during the war was complete. But even given a more prompt solution of these difficult problems, the rehabilitation of the economic structure of Europe quite evidently will require a much longer time and greater effort than bad been foreseen.

Source 4
Excerpt from Marshall Speech (1947)

The farmer has always produced the foodstuffs to exchange with the city dweller for the other necessities of life. This division of labor is the basis of modern civilization. At the present time it is threatened with breakdown. The town and city industries are not producing adequate goods to exchange with the food-producing farmer. Raw materials and fuel are in short supply. Machinery is lacking or worn out. The farmer or the peasant cannot find the goods for sale which he desires to purchase. So the sale of his farm produce for money which he cannot use seems to him an unprofitable transaction.

Source 5
Excerpt from Marshall Speech (1947)

Aside from the demoralizing effect on the world at large and the possibilities of disturbances arising as a result of the desperation of the people concerned, the consequences to the economy of the United States should be apparent to all.

Source 6
Excerpt from Marshall Speech (1947)

The truth of the matter is that Europe's requirements for the next three or four years of foreign food and other essential products— principally from America—are so much greater than her present ability to pay that she must have substantial additional help or face economic, social, and political deterioration of a very grave character.

Source 7
Excerpt from Atlantic Charter (1941)

The President of the United States of America and the Prime Minister, Mr. Churchill, representing His Majesty's Government in the United Kingdom, being met together, deem it right to make known certain common principles in the national policies of their respective countries on which they base their hopes for a better future for the world:

. . . They respect the right of all peoples to choose the form of government under which they will live; and they wish to see sovereign rights and self government restored to those who have been forcibly deprived of them;

. . . They desire to bring about the fullest collaboration between all nations in the economic field with the object of securing, for all, improved labor standards, economic advancement and social security.

Source 8
Excerpt from Atlantic Charter (1941)

The President of the United States of America and the Prime Minister,
Mr. Churchill, representing His Majesty's Government in the United
Kingdom, being met together, deem it right to make known certain
common principles in the national policies of their respective countries
on which they base their hopes for a better future for the world:

. . . After the final destruction of the Nazi tyranny, they hope to see
established a peace which will afford to all nations the means of
dwelling in safety within their own boundaries, and which will afford
assurance that all the men in all lands may live out their lives in
freedom from fear and want;

. . . They believe that all of the nations of the world, for realistic as well
as spiritual reasons must come to the abandonment of the use of force.
Since no future peace can be maintained if land, sea or air armaments
continue to be employed by nations which threaten, or may threaten,
aggression outside of their frontiers, they believe, pending the establishment of a wider and permanent system of general security, that the
disarmament of such nations is essential.

Source 9
Map of Europe Showing Iron Curtain

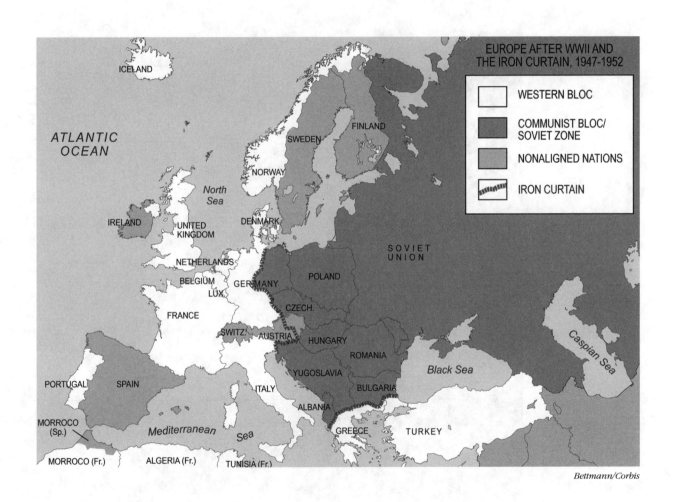

EUROPE AFTER WWII AND
THE IRON CURTAIN, 1947-1952

WESTERN BLOC

COMMUNIST BLOC/
SOVIET ZONE

NONALIGNED NATIONS

IRON CURTAIN

ICELAND

ATLANTIC
OCEAN

FINLAND

SWEDEN

NORWAY

North
Sea

IRELAND

UNITED
KINGDOM

DENMARK

SOVIET
UNION

NETHERLANDS

BELGIUM

GERMANY

POLAND

LUX.

CZECH.

FRANCE

SWITZ.

AUSTRIA

HUNGARY

Caspian
Sea

ROMANIA

YUGOSLAVIA

Black Sea

PORTUGAL

SPAIN

ITALY

BULGARIA

MORROCO
(Sp.)

ALBANIA

Mediterranean   Sea

GREECE

TURKEY

MORROCO (Fr.)

ALGERIA (Fr.)

TUNISIA (Fr.)

This map shows Europe
at the beginning of the
Cold War, as the world
began to divide into
alliances with Communist
or Democratic powers.

Source 10
Photo of Dresden (1945)

View of the wreckage of Dresden, Germany, after the Allies fire-bombed it in 1945. The bombing, which targeted the civilian population, was one of the most devastating aerial raids in history. Four years after the blaze, the city still appeared as a wasteland; most of its buildings were gutted, including many 1,000-year-old structures that were completely destroyed. It took Germany decades to rebuild the city of Dresden.

Library of Congress

Source 11
Photo of Nuremberg (1944)

National Archives

By the autumn of 1944, such German industrial cities as Nuremberg were being bombed night and day by American and British forces. Nuremberg, which was vital to the Nazis as an industrial center, was captured by U.S. troops on April 20, 1945.

Source 12
Photo of Hamburg (1943)

Library of Congress

Bombed buildings in Hamburg, Germany, in July, 1943. In response to Germany's leveling of Coventry, the British Royal Air Force bombed Hamburg in a series of attacks that ultimately created a firestorm that killed more than 40,000 civilians. This series of air raids was called Operation GOMORRAH.

Source 13
Excerpts from Marshall Speech (1947)

The remedy lies in breaking the vicious circle and restoring the confidence of the European people in the economic future of their own countries and of Europe as a whole. The manufacturer and the farmer throughout wide areas must be able and willing to exchange their products for currencies the continuing value of which is not open to question. . . .

It is logical that the United States should do whatever it is able to do to assist in the return of normal economic health in the world, without which there can be no political stability and no assured peace. . . .

Our policy is directed not against any country or doctrine but against hunger, poverty, desperation, and chaos. Its purpose should be the revival of a working economy in the world so as to permit the emergence of political and social conditions in which free institutions can exist. . . .

Any government which maneuvers to block the recovery of other countries cannot expect help from us. Furthermore, governments, political parties, or groups which seek to perpetuate human misery in order to profit there from politically or otherwise will encounter the opposition of the United States. . . .

Source 13
Excerpts from Marshall Speech (1947), cont.

The initiative, I think, must come from Europe. The role of [the United States] should consist of friendly aid in the drafting of a European program and of later support of such a program so far as it may be practical for us to do so . . .

An essential part of any successful action on the part of the United States is an understanding on the part of the people of America of the character of the problem and the remedies to be applied. Political passion and prejudice should have no part. With foresight, and a willingness on the part of our people to face up to the vast responsibility which history has clearly placed upon our country, the difficulties I have outlined can and will be overcome . . .

Political Cartoon 1A

Courtesy Donald E. Marcus and Family

Political Cartoon 2A

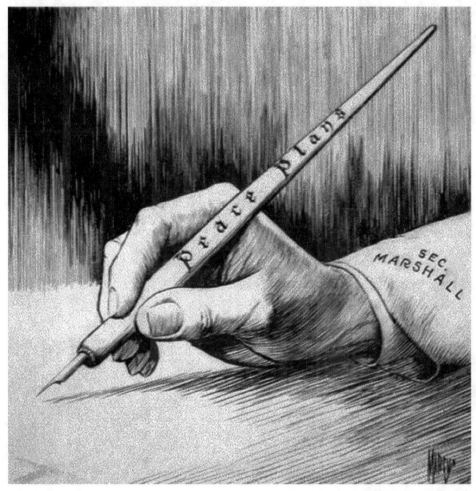

Courtesy Donald E. Marcus and Family

Political Cartoon 3A

Political Cartoon 4A

Courtesy Donald E. Marcus and Family

Political Cartoon 5A

Courtesy Donald E. Marcus and Family

Political Cartoon 6A

Courtesy Donald E. Marcus and Family

Political Cartoon 7A

Courtesy Herb Block Foundation

Political Cartoon 8A

Courtesy Donald E. Marcus and Family

Political Cartoon 1B

Courtesy Donald E. Marcus and Family

Cartoon shows an apprehensive man (labeled "Western Europe") looking toward
the U.S. Capitol (labeled "Marshall Plan Delay") while in the foreground the huge
menacing shadow of a bear looms. The cartoon suggests that the delay in
approving the plan to provide economic aid to the war-impoverished countries of
Europe puts them in danger of Soviet domination. Congress finally approved the
plan in April, 1948, eleven months after it was originally proposed.

Political Cartoon 2B

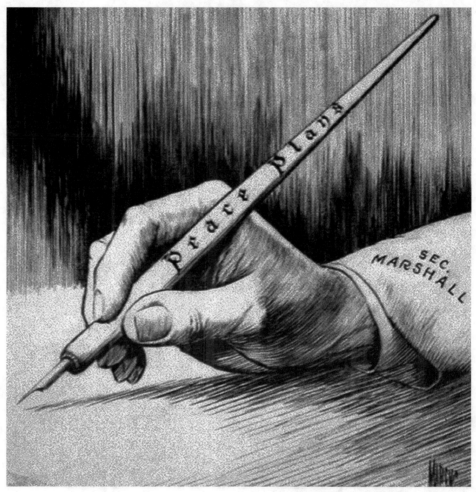

Courtesy Donald E. Marcus and Family

Cartoon shows the hand of Secretary of State George C. Marshall holding a pen labeled "Peace Plans." It expresses the hope that the newly appointed secretary of state will be as successful in his diplomatic role as he had been as army chief of staff during World War II.

Political Cartoon 3B

Library of Congress

Cartoon shows a huge parade of marchers, with dollar coins for heads and banners reading "Ten Billion Strong" and "Lafayette, we are here," marching under the Arch de Triomphe. Making a comparison to the arrival in France of American troops, with their slogans, to help the Allies during World War I, cynically comments on massive American economic aid to France after World War II.

Political Cartoon 4B

Courtesy Donald E. Marcus and Family

Cartoon shows a man labeled "Italy" setting an old-fashioned clock which has the words "European Recovery" rather than numbers. Drawn as Americans reset their clocks for Daylight Saving Time, the cartoon comments on the success of the European Recovery Program in promoting economic recovery in Italy after World War II.

Political Cartoon 5B

Courtesy Donald E. Marcus and Family

Cartoon shows a haughty waiter, labeled

"Congress" carrying a tray labeled "Aid to

Europe Plan," heading for a banana peel

labeled "Politics."

Political Cartoon 6B

Courtesy Donald E. Marcus and Family

Cartoon shows the booted legs of a man, labeled "West Europe," walking across a body of water on stepping stones toward "Recovery."

Political Cartoon 7B

Courtesy Herb Block Foundation

Editorial cartoon showing a Russian man yoked to a plow and turning the soil of the "Marshal Stalin Plan," as Joseph Stalin tries to persuade other Russians that "it's the same thing without mechanical problems"; in the background, a man rides on a new tractor "Marshall Plan."

Political Cartoon 8B

Courtesy Donald E. Marcus and Family

Cartoon shows Soviet leader Joseph Stalin as a
basketball player trying to block a ball labeled
"Marshall Plan" from a basket labeled "European
recovery." Probably drawn in 1947 as the Russians
vainly tried to prevent the Western European nations
from accepting U.S. aid through the Marshall Plan.

Image 1
Photo of Berlin

National Archives

A worker shovels rubble during the rebuilding of West Berlin in front of a building adorned with a sign supporting the Marshall Plan. Introduced by the United States in 1947, the massive financial aid program allowed Germany not only to rebuild, but to surpass its prewar industrial production level.

Image 2
Photo of Poster

1947: two men in front of a poster supporting the European Recovery Plan, also known as the Marshall Plan after the U.S. Secretary of State George Marshall.

Getty Images

Image 3
Emblem of European Recovery Program (ERP)

Bettmann/Corbis

The European Recovery Program (ERP) emblem was stamped on every relief package sent abroad as part of the Marshall Plan.

Image 4
Poster for Marshall Plan

Poster promoting
the Marshall Plan
has the title "Peace
without Fear."

Library of Congress

Image 5
Poster for Marshall Plan

Poster supporting the
Marshall Plan is titled
"Whatever the weather
we only reach welfare
together."

Swim Ink 2, LLC/Corbis

Image 6
Poster for Marshall Plan

Poster of a ship with sails depicting the many nations involved in the Marshall Plan.

Library of Congress

Image 7
Resource Allotment Map of Europe

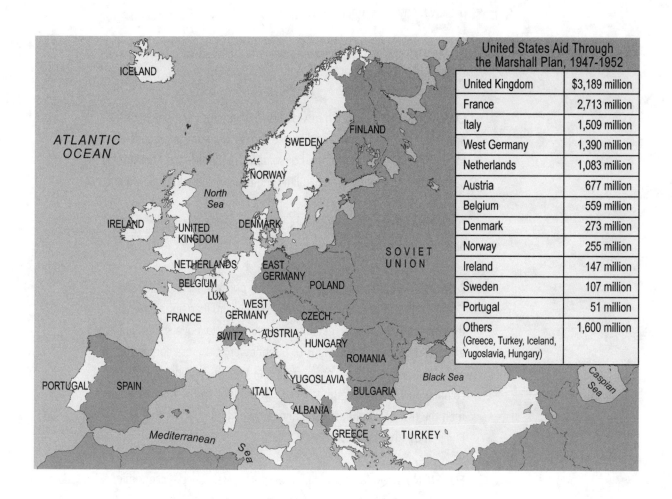

United States Aid Through the Marshall Plan, 1947-1952	
United Kingdom	$3,189 million
France	2,713 million
Italy	1,509 million
West Germany	1,390 million
Netherlands	1,083 million
Austria	677 million
Belgium	559 million
Denmark	273 million
Norway	255 million
Ireland	147 million
Sweden	107 million
Portugal	51 million
Others (Greece, Turkey, Iceland, Yugoslavia, Hungary)	1,600 million

Map of Europe showing nations that received aid under the Marshall Plan, with a chart showing amounts each received.

Glossary Words, Ideas, or Movements
Building Alliances, Combating Communism,
and Fostering Recovery

CAPITALISM A free-enterprise system that stresses private ownership of most farms and industries as a means of economic growth and the preservation of personal liberty.

COMMUNISM A social system in which a classless society owns and shares all property as a whole.

CONTAINMENT A policy that was first implemented by the United States in 1947 in response to Communism. It is meant to prevent—through political, economic, and diplomatic methods—the growth of a hostile country's territory and to limit the country's ideological influence.

DISARMAMENT Generally refers to the reduction, limitation, or abolition of a nation's weapons and armaments.

DOMINO THEORY The view held by U.S. policy makers during the Cold War that if one country fell to Communism, its neighbors were threatened with a chain reaction of Communist takeovers. First publicly expressed by President Dwight D. Eisenhower at a press conference in 1954, the domino theory arose from fear that the withdrawal of colonial powers from Southeast Asia would lead to the fall of Vietnam, then the rest of Southeast Asia, and perhaps India, Japan, the Philippines, and Indonesia.

FOREIGN AID Refers to any kind of official assistance—economic, social, or military—offered to a country, organization, or cause. Such help is provided by a nation, a group of nations, or an international organization and may include donations of food or money, development loans, technical help, or military support. Governments may also provide foreign aid to states, provinces, or organizations to help with education, social welfare, or other needs.

FOREIGN POLICY Comprises a country's goals in relation to other nations and the methods and strategies used to achieve them, including diplomacy, technical assistance, and economic aid.

SELF-GOVERNMENT Refers to a state of political independence and autonomy in which governmental power is not controlled by an outside authority.

SOVEREIGNTY A state's supreme authority to govern itself. When one government recognizes the sovereignty of another, it recognizes that government's right to rule over a designated territory and to exist as an independent nation, equal to all other sovereign nations in the international community.

SOVIET BLOC The group name for the Eastern European nations, including such countries as Albania, Bulgaria, Czechoslovakia, East Germany, Hungary, Poland, and Romania, that installed Communist governments after World War II.

Biographies and Organizations
Building Alliances, Combating Communism, and Fostering Recovery

NATO Photos

ACHESON, DEAN

Secretary of State Dean Acheson signs the North Atlantic Treaty on behalf of the United States on April 4, 1949.

As secretary of state from 1949 to 1953, Dean Gooderham Acheson helped create the North Atlantic Treaty Organization (NATO), engineered a 1951 peace treaty with Japan, and implemented President Harry Truman's policies in Korea.

Born on April 11, 1893 in Middletown, Connecticut, Acheson graduated from Yale University in 1915. He earned his law degree from Harvard Law School in 1918 after briefly serving in the U.S. Navy during World War I. From 1919 to 1921, Acheson was Supreme Court Justice Louis Brandeis' private secretary. Except for a brief stint as President Franklin D. Roosevelt's under secretary of the treasury in 1933, Acheson practiced corporate and international law from 1921 to 1941.

Appointed by Roosevelt as assistant secretary of state in 1941, Acheson helped secure congressional passage of the Lend-Lease Act and later of the Bretton Woods Monetary Agreement. As under secretary of state from 1945 to 1947, Acheson played a vital role in the formulation of the Truman Doctrine in 1947, which pledged the United States to the worldwide containment of Communism. He also worked closely with George Marshall in devising the Marshall Plan, a massive economic aid program designed to promote the recovery of the European economies and thus thwart the appeal of Communism.

In 1949, Truman selected Acheson as the new secretary of state. Acheson's two greatest accomplishments involved the creation of NATO and the conclusion of a peace treaty with Japan in 1951. Although a staunch opponent of Communism who believed that it was "economically fatal to a free society and to human rights and fundamental freedom," Acheson, like his mentor, George Marshall, became the target of Republican critics, who virulently and unfairly attacked him for "losing" China to the Communists. Acheson's critics assailed him for encouraging the Communist North Koreans to invade South Korea in 1950, thereby involving the United States in a costly and inconclusive four-year war. Part of what made him politically vulnerable to these charges was the perception of many mainstream Americans that he belonged to an Eastern establishment whose internationalism, elitism, and New Deal liberalism were out of step with basic American values.

After leaving office at the end of the Truman administration, Acheson returned to his law practice, wrote books on international diplomacy, and served as an unofficial policy adviser to presidents. He died on October 12, 1971.

Biographies and Organizations
Building Alliances, Combating Communism,
and Fostering Recovery, cont.

CHURCHILL, WINSTON

Library of Congress

Soviet leader Josef Stalin (left), U.S. President Franklin D. Roosevelt (center), British Prime Minister Winston Churchill (right), and various military officers meet on the portico of the Russian Embassy in Tehran, Iran, in 1943. The conference, which was held from November, 28 to December 1, 1943, was a meeting of the Big Three to discuss the strategy of the Allies during World War II.

In a versatile career that spanned four decades, Winston Leonard Spencer Churchill served Great Britain as a soldier, politician, member of the British Parliament, first lord of the Admiralty, and prime minister. A prolific writer and an eloquent orator as well, he inspired Britons with his writings and speeches during the dark days of World War II. A man of action as well as a man of words, he was an inspiring and decisive military and political leader during both world wars.

Churchill was born at Blenheim Palace, Woodstock, Oxfordshire, on November 30, 1874. In 1893, he qualified with difficulty to attend Sandhurst Royal Military College as a cavalry cadet. After graduating in 1894, he was commissioned in the British Army and joined the Fourth Hussars. In 1900, Churchill became a member of Parliament for Oldham, standing with the British Conservative Party.

He was appointed president of the Board of Trade in 1908, and in 1910 became home secretary, one of the most powerful positions in the government. In 1911, Churchill was appointed first lord of the Admiralty, a position that seemed a perfect match for Churchill's talents and interests. However, in the aftermath of public criticism over the Dardanelles and Gallipoli campaigns during World War I, Churchill was removed as first lord of the Admiralty.

After the war ended in November, 1918, Churchill held a series of government positions in which he supervised demobilization. In 1921, he became colonial secretary. He was defeated in his bid for parliamentary office in 1922, but in October, 1924, he was elected for Epping. He was subsequently appointed chancellor of the exchequer under Prime Minister Stanley Baldwin. Churchill's tenure as chancellor, however, was marked by national unrest and economic instability, and he left office in 1929.

Throughout the 1930s, Churchill became increasingly angry at the government's unwillingness to recognize the threat posed by the rise of fascism in Europe in general and the establishment of the Nazi Party in Germany in particular. He became an outspoken opponent of Prime Minister Neville Chamberlain's policy of appeasement toward German dictator Adolf Hitler. When World War II began in September, 1939, Churchill returned to politics once again as first lord of the Admiralty. In May, 1940, after Chamberlain resigned the premiership, Churchill formed a coalition government and became prime minister.

At that point, Britain was facing what many believed was the country's darkest hour. Paris had been captured by the Nazis, and all of France was on the point of capitulation to the Germans. Few doubted that Hitler would turn his attention to Britain next. Churchill appeared to meet the German threat without fear, and he rallied the British people to what he called the ultimate fight for survival. His leadership would prove vital to the British war effort and empowered the country to stave off the threat of invasion and conquest. By 1944, the Allies had built up their own strength and weakened the Germans enough that Churchill gave his support to an invasion of France. He played an instrumental role in organizing the resulting D-Day operation in June of that year, which ultimately led to the liberation of Western Europe and the defeat of Germany.

Biographies and Organizations
Building Alliances, Combating Communism, and Fostering Recovery, cont.

With victory for the Allies in sight, Churchill turned his attention increasingly to the shape of the postwar world. Through a series of conferences, Churchill, U.S. President Franklin D. Roosevelt, and Soviet leader Joseph Stalin hammered out tentative agreements for dealing with a defeated Germany and restoring order to the world. Earlier than his colleagues, Churchill perceived the great struggle between Communism and Democracy that emerged as the Cold War began in 1945 and would dominate world affairs for more than the next forty years.

Churchill received another blow in July, 1945, when the Conservatives were defeated in the general election. He became the leader of the opposition in Parliament, a cruel disappointment after his wartime prestige. He remained, however, an international hero and proved himself an astute observer of worldwide affairs. In 1953, Churchill suffered his third and most serious stroke. He continued in office for two more years, however, resigning on April 5, 1955. He formally retired from the House of Commons in July, 1964. Churchill died in London on January 24, 1965.

KENNAN, GEORGE F.

Library of Congress

American politician George F. Kennan in 1951. In a famous memorandum cabled from Moscow in 1947, Kennan defined the central goal of U.S. foreign policy during the Cold War: containment of the Soviet Union in its postwar sphere of influence.

In a famous memorandum cabled from Moscow and published anonymously in *Foreign Affairs* in July, 1947, George Frost Kennan defined the central goal of U.S. foreign policy during the Cold War: containment of the Soviet Union in its postwar sphere of influence. Kennan's recommendation provided the rationale for the Truman Doctrine, the Marshall Plan, and the North Atlantic Treaty Organization (NATO).

Kennan was born on February 16, 1904, in Milwaukee, Wisconsin. He graduated from Princeton University in 1925 and entered the U.S. foreign service the next year. From 1929 until 1931, Kennan studied Russian language, culture, and history at the Berlin Seminar for Oriental Languages and the University of Berlin through a special program designed to provide the State Department with experts on the Soviet Union. During the 1930s, Kennan completed tours of duty in Moscow, Vienna, and Prague. From May, 1944 to April, 1946, he was minister-counselor in Moscow. Upon his return to the United States in 1946, Kennan became a lecturer on foreign policy issues at the National War College in Washington, D.C. for a year, then director of the policy-planning staff of the State Department responsible for long-range planning of U.S. action in foreign affairs. It was at that time that his article advocating the containment of the Soviet Union's expansionist efforts, signed by "X" was published in the journal *Foreign Affairs*.

From 1949 until his appointment as ambassador to the Soviet Union in 1952, Kennan was one of Secretary of State Dean Acheson's principal advisers. He served less than a year in Moscow as ambassador before the Soviet government demanded his replacement because he had spoken out against the treatment of diplomats in the Soviet Union. Kennan left the foreign service in 1953 to accept a faculty appointment at the Institute for Advanced Study at Princeton.

In a series of lectures in 1957, Kennan attacked what he viewed as a perversion of his containment policy toward the Soviet Union into a dangerous military confrontational situation that exposed the world to nuclear devastation. He advocated a policy of coexistence with the Soviet Union based upon a realistic assessment of the respective power and interests of that country and the United States.

Biographies and Organizations
Building Alliances, Combating Communism, and Fostering Recovery, cont.

During the next two decades, through numerous speeches, lectures, and publications, Kennan offered a number of controversial foreign policy suggestions that eventually came to be shared by many Americans. They included the mutual withdrawal of U.S. and Soviet troops from Europe, the reunification of Germany as a neutral nation, the avoidance of involvement in Vietnam, the abolishment of nuclear weapons, and the protection of the environment from the ravages of industrialization.

After he received the Presidential Medal of Freedom in 1989, Kennan withdrew from public life. He died at his home in Princeton, New Jersey, on March 17, 2005.

LOVETT, ROBERT

One of the most important architects of American diplomatic and defense policies after World War II, Robert Lovett developed most of the details of the Marshall Plan that rebuilt Europe. He contributed to the creation of the North American Treaty Organization (NATO) and served as an unofficial adviser to presidents John F. Kennedy and Lyndon B. Johnson.

Hulton Archive/Getty Images

Robert Abercrombie Lovett served as U.S. undersecretary of state and secretary of defense during the Korean War. He also played an important role in the Marshall Plan and in the creation of the North Atlantic Treaty Organization (NATO).

Born on September 14, 1895 in Huntsville, Texas, Lovett attended Yale University. After graduating, he entered Harvard law and business schools before joining the Wall Street investment banking firm of Brown Brothers. In 1926, he became a partner, and during the remaining interwar years, Lovett concentrated on international investment and banking matters.

As a champion of air power, Lovett wrote a study in 1940 on airplane production that caught the attention of Secretary of War Henry L. Stimson. In particular, Lovett's recommendations that the United States should be increasing its aircraft production to meet what he saw as the growing German threat led to his appointment as a special assistant to the secretary of war from December, 1940 to April, 1941 and then assistant secretary of war for air thereafter. Throughout World War II, Lovett had the ear of U.S. Army Chief of Staff General George C. Marshall and probably did more than any other man to bring the United States into the modern age of air power.

After the war, Lovett returned to investment banking, but in 1947, his close friend Secretary of State Marshall recalled him to government service to serve as undersecretary of state. In this position, Lovett worked to secure congressional approval for the Marshall Plan, the rehabilitation of Germany, and the creation of NATO. Lovett also helped to plan the Berlin airlift. When Marshall resigned as secretary of state in 1949, Lovett also left government service, returning to his law practice.

During the Korean War, when Louis A. Johnson was replaced as secretary of defense, Lovett rejoined Marshall, Johnson's replacement, as undersecretary of defense in September, 1950. When Marshall resigned in September, 1951 for reasons of ill health, President Harry S. Truman nominated Lovett as Marshall's successor. As secretary of defense from 1951 until 1953, Lovett expanded missile development programs and research into chemical and biological weapons. He was also a strong advocate of conscription and a coordinated defense budget.

After Dwight Eisenhower's inauguration as president in 1953, Lovett returned to banking and became the chief executive officer of the Union Pacific Railroad. He later acted as an unofficial adviser both to President John F. Kennedy and to President Lyndon B. Johnson. Lovett died in Locust Valley, New York, on May 7, 1986.

Biographies and Organizations
Building Alliances, Combating Communism,
and Fostering Recovery, cont.

Library of Congress

MARSHALL, GEORGE C.

*General George C. Marshall was the U.S. Army chief of staff
from 1939 to 1945. Marshall developed the central strategy for
all Allied operations in Europe, selected Dwight Eisenhower as
supreme commander in Europe, and designed Operation
OVERLORD, the invasion of Normandy. Throughout the
remainder of World War II, Marshall coordinated all Allied
operations in Europe and the Pacific.*

On September 1, 1939, the day World War II officially began in
Europe, George Catlett Marshall became chief of staff of the
U.S. Army. For the next twelve years, first as chief of staff and then as
secretary of state, Marshall played a vital role in the military and
political events that shaped the modern world.

Born on December 31, 1880 in Uniontown, Pennsylvania, Marshall
began his army career in 1902 after graduating from the Virginia
Military Institute. He served in the Philippines from 1902 to 1903 and
then again from 1913 to 1916. In 1917, he went to France, where he
helped to plan the first U.S. campaigns in the war. Then, transferred to
general headquarters, he was instrumental in plotting the successful
strategy of the Saint-Mihiel and Meuse-Argonne offensives as First
Army chief of operations. With the exception of the period 1924 to
1927, when he was executive officer of an infantry regiment in China,
Marshall served from 1919 to 1938 in a variety of capacities at various
military bases around the United States.

Impressed by reports of Marshall's administrative skills and extraordinary ability to recognize talent, President Franklin D. Roosevelt selected Marshall over thirty-four senior officers to be army chief of staff. Marshall occupied the position from 1939 to 1945. Marshall was the principal military strategist for all Allied operations in Europe and the Pacific during World War II.

After the war, President Harry Truman asked Marshall to undertake what turned out to be the hopeless task of trying to arrange some kind of negotiated peace between the Nationalist and Communist forces in China. As Truman's secretary of state from 1947 to 1949, Marshall, who believed the Soviets were bent on controlling Europe, helped the president to formulate his containment policy. Convinced that economic instability aided Soviet Communist expansion, Marshall outlined, in a speech delivered at Harvard University in June, 1947, a plan by which the United States would help to ensure Europe's economic recovery. He proposed that during the next several years, the United States ought to help Europe with substantial grants and loans to prevent "economic, social, and political deterioration of very grave character."

The Marshall Plan was signed into law in April, 1948, and $5.3 billion in aid was provided to Europe the following year. Of the $12 billion spent in Marshall aid, more than half went to Great Britain, France, and West Germany. By 1950, these nations had increased their gross national products by more than twenty-five percent. Their prosperity did help to contain Communism, and as they became more prosperous, they bought more U.S. goods. Acceptance of Marshall aid bound recipients to make all their purchases in the United States and European Commonwealth countries. This restriction helped to fuel the postwar U.S. economic prosperity. U.S. policy makers would often refer to the success of the Marshall Plan to support aid programs for Asia, Latin America, and Africa.

Biographies and Organizations
Building Alliances, Combating Communism, and Fostering Recovery, cont.

Marshall resigned as secretary of state because of ill health in 1949, but President Truman asked him to return as secretary of defense at the outbreak of the Korean War in 1950. As secretary of defense from 1950 to 1951, Marshall rebuilt the armed forces, devised a plan for universal military training, helped create the North Atlantic Treaty Organization (NATO), and successfully worked to keep the Korean War contained to the Korean peninsula.

In 1953, shortly after his retirement, in recognition of his efforts to end and to avert war around the world, Marshall became the only professional soldier ever awarded the Nobel Peace Prize. He died six years later on October 16, 1959.

ROOSEVELT, FRANKLIN D.

Corel

British Prime Minister Winston Churchill (left), U.S. President Franklin D. Roosevelt (center), and an unidentified officer stand together on the HMS Prince of Wales on August 14, 1941. The meeting aboard the British ship was called to set forth the principles of and sign the Atlantic Charter, a document that articulated joint U.S.–British goals for fostering international peace and mutual security.

Former governor of New York and thirty-second president of the United States, Franklin Delano Roosevelt's presidency spanned the turbulent years of the Great Depression and World War II.

Roosevelt was born at Hyde Park, New York, on January 30, 1882. He graduated from Harvard University in 1904 and then studied at Columbia University law school before beginning his career as a lawyer. In 1905, Roosevelt married a distant cousin, Eleanor Roosevelt.

Roosevelt began his political career in 1910 when he successfully ran
for the New York Senate. In 1912, he supported Democratic candidate
Woodrow Wilson for the presidency. Wilson appointed him assistant
secretary of the navy in 1913, and Roosevelt continued in that post
until 1920, serving throughout World War I. In 1920, he ran as the
Democratic vice presidential candidate on the party ticket with James
M. Cox, but they lost to Warren Harding and Calvin Coolidge. After he
returned to New York, Roosevelt contracted polio, which left him
crippled. He spent the next eight years working to regain the use of his
legs and reemerged on the political scene in 1928, to win the gover-
norship of New York. In 1932, he successfully ran for president against
Republican incumbent Herbert Hoover. By this time, the country had
been in a serious economic depression for three years.

When Roosevelt became president, the Great Depression was in full
swing. Roosevelt's approach to economic policy embodied both experi-
mentation and pragmatism and was not a total break with Hoover's
policies. The U.S. Supreme Court declared much of this early New Deal
legislation, which was meant to restart the depressed economy, uncon-
stitutional in 1935. But the Court came around to the New Deal-style
of thinking by 1937 and began upholding measures such as the
National Labor Relations Act of 1935.

In foreign relations, Roosevelt initiated the Good Neighbor Policy with
Central and South America in an effort to open trade within the
Western Hemisphere. He enjoyed less success in economically
depressed Europe, where Adolf Hitler was already in control of
Germany. When World War II broke out, Roosevelt tried to maintain
American neutrality, which was required under the Neutrality Acts of
1935 and 1936 that forbid the sale of arms or the lending of funds to
belligerent nations. After the fall of France and the bombing of England
by Germany, Roosevelt implemented a new program called Lend-Lease
that allowed the British and Russians to obtain goods without paying
for them immediately.

Biographies and Organizations
Building Alliances, Combating Communism,
and Fostering Recovery, cont.

By that time, the United States was on the verge of entering the war. In August, 1941, Roosevelt and British Prime Minister Winston Churchill issued a joint statement, the Atlantic Charter, in which they pledged the shared goal of destroying "Nazi tyranny" and affirming national self-determination for all nations. After the Japanese attack on Pearl Harbor on December 7, 1941, the United States quickly declared war on Japan. On April 12, 1945, Roosevelt died in Warm Springs, Georgia, just a few weeks before Germany surrendered and four months before the capitulation of Japan.

Library of Congress

TRUMAN, HARRY S

Harry S Truman, president of the United States from 1945 until 1953. Truman led the United States through the end of World War II and the beginning of the Cold War. While seen as a failure during his term, Truman has been lauded as one of the nation's greatest presidents.

Harry Truman, often referred to as "Give 'em hell Harry" because of his forthright manner, became president of the United States at the end of World War II and helped to shape the postwar world.

Born on May 8, 1884, Truman grew up on a farm near Independence, Missouri. During World War I, he served as an artillery officer in France, rising to the rank of captain. In 1934, Missouri political boss Tom Pendergast, looking for a "man of unimpeachable character and integrity" to restore the image of his political machine, helped Truman win election to the U.S. Senate. He was reelected in 1940, and by 1944, when President Franklin D. Roosevelt chose him to be his fourth-term running mate, Truman was a respected figure in the Senate.

Truman assumed the office of president after the unexpected death of
Roosevelt on April 12, 1945. He became president during an extraordi-
narily difficult period with very little preparation. During his first two
years in office, Truman had to confront the immensely difficult tasks of
rebuilding the nations ravaged by World War II and containing the
powerful appeal of Communism. He had to negotiate the future of the
U.S. and Soviet presence in Europe and the Middle East with Joseph
Stalin, decide whether to use the atomic bomb to end the war with
Japan, confront Soviet domination of Eastern Europe, cope with
massive labor unrest and postwar inflation in the United States, and
deal with a hostile, newly elected Republican Congress.

Truman was in an awkward political position in 1947. He was viewed
as antilabor by unions and antibusiness by executives because of his
support of wage and price controls. He was also unpopular in the South
because he favored civil rights legislation and in the Northeast because
of his unsophisticated demeanor. Stymied on the domestic front, he
moved boldly in the international arena to contain Communism. The
Truman Doctrine of 1947 declared the determination of the United States
to use its military might to contain Communism and fight Communist
insurgencies in every corner of the world. Among the many programs
Truman initiated through bipartisan foreign policy support in Congress
were the Marshall Plan and the creation of the North Atlantic Treaty
Organization (NATO).

Biographies and Organizations
Building Alliances, Combating Communism, and Fostering Recovery, cont.

Truman won the 1948 presidential election by a narrow margin over Republican candidate Thomas E. Dewey in a stunning political upset. Truman's second term was dominated by a period of mass hysteria over fears that Communist spies were infiltrating America and by the Korean War. Plagued by dwindling popular support and charges of governmental corruption, Truman decided not to run for reelection in 1952. He subsequently was snubbed by the newly elected Dwight D. Eisenhower during his inauguration ceremony and judged a failure as president by contemporaries. Truman's reputation began to improve during the eight years of the boring and allegedly ineffectual Eisenhower administration. By 1960 and the return of the Democrats to the White House, Truman's good reputation had been restored.

Truman spent the last two decades of his life writing his memoirs, establishing the Truman Library, and traveling. He died on December 26, 1972.

ECONOMIC COOPERATION ADMINISTRATION (ECA)

The ECA was a U.S. agency created by the Economic Recovery Act of April, 1948 to administer postwar American aid to Western Europe under the Marshall Plan.

The Marshall Plan, announced by U.S. Secretary of State General George C. Marshall on June 5, 1947, sought to stabilize Europe politically and to help Western European economies recover by integrating them into a U.S–dominated international economic order. Before the creation of ECA in July, 1947, sixteen Western European nations created the Committee of European Economic Cooperation, later renamed Organization for European Economic Cooperation (OEEC), a body charged with assembling a coordinated proposal for the use of funds in Europe. Throughout the autumn and winter of 1947, the U.S. administration and Congress discussed the best way to help Western Europe and decided to grant both interim and long-term aid. Congress approved the European Recovery Program (ERP) on April 3, 1948, and called for the plan to be administered by the ECA, the government oversight agency, and the OEEC, which would actually distribute funds in Europe. Over the next four years, the ECA administered $12 billion in aid.

The ECA administrators encompassed both liberal academics, politicians working according to Keynesian ideas, and forward-looking businesspeople like ECA's first administrator, Paul Hoffmann. He hoped to modernize the Western European economies and help them to recover, both to support social stability and to shape a continent-sized market. In turn, setting up intra-European trade would have reduced Europe's need for American aid and increased European productivity. However, European nations did not see the OEEC as a supranational body that would distribute aid across the continent on a rational basis and improve national economies by building intra-European trade. Instead, each European nation tended to help its own economy to recover by using OEEC funds within its own nation.

In 1951, Congress replaced the ECA with the Mutual Security Agency (MSA), which had an aid policy aimed at increasing military supplies and coordinating economic and military plans. The MSA was abolished in 1953 when its functions were transferred to the Foreign Operations Administration.

BACKGROUND
MATERIAL

Biographies and Organizations
Building Alliances, Combating Communism,
and Fostering Recovery, cont.

COMMITTEE OF EUROPEAN ECONOMIC COOPERATION

I n July, 1947, sixteen Western European nations created the Committee of European Economic Cooperation, later renamed Organization for European Economic Cooperation (OEEC), a body charged with assembling a coordinated proposal for the use of foreign aid in postwar Europe.

The OEEC basically distributed two kinds of aid—on one hand a great number of direct grants (food, fertilizer, machinery, shipping, raw materials, and fuel) and on the other the equivalent of more than $4.3 billion in counterpart funds—that is, the local currency receipt of sales of foreign aid material on national markets. These currency receipts were placed in a special fund used to invest in the industrial sector and aid the recovery of European infrastructure.

COUNCIL OF MUTUAL ECONOMIC ASSISTANCE (COMECON)

I n an effort to counter the growing political and economic cooperation of the countries of Western Europe, the Soviet Union and the Communist states of Eastern Europe formed the Council of Mutual Economic Assistance (Comecon) in 1949. Comecon served as the vehicle to allow the Soviet satellite states to coordinate their planned economies. However, Comecon was not very effective and its importance declined as time passed.

Comecon had its beginnings as Western Europe began its movement toward economic integration shortly after World War II. In 1948, the Western states formed the Committee of European Economic Cooperation. Integration quickly proved to be a success, and the "economic miracle" dramatically raised standards of living throughout the region. The Soviet Union hoped to counter this development with an integrationist movement of its own. In 1949, the states of Albania, Bulgaria, Czechoslovakia, Hungary, Poland, Romania, and the Soviet Union reached the basic agreement that formed Comecon. The final charter of the organization was delayed, and formal ratification occurred in 1959. Comecon attempted to create conditions whereby its members, working together, could achieve complete economic self-sufficiency for the Soviet bloc. Because each Communist state employed a planned economy, the idea was to coordinate the planning among the members to increase productivity and the distribution of goods. Comecon employed the five-year plan as the basis for its activity. The council attempted to develop five-year plans that met specific production goals.

The membership of Comecon grew and became more diverse with time. East Germany joined in 1950. Mongolia followed in 1962. Cuba and Vietnam joined in 1972 and 1978, respectively. Albania withdrew in 1961.

Comecon met with limited success. The first fifteen years of the organization produced a 400 percent increase in trade among the member states. But after 1964, trade began a slow but steady decline. Comecon was most successful in establishing infrastructure. It sponsored the

Biographies and Organizations
Building Alliances, Combating Communism, and Fostering Recovery, cont.

building of the first major oil pipeline from Russia to Eastern Europe. Under Comecon's leadership, the railroad network and power grid of the region were upgraded. In 1963, Comecon created the International Bank for Economic Cooperation.

Comecon failed in its attempts for self-sufficiency because it had limited power to affect change within its member states. In particular, the pricing systems of each command economy were completely arbitrary and conflicting. Thus, no satisfactory pricing system for the trade of goods across borders developed.

With the collapse of Communism across Eastern Europe in 1989, Comecon mutated. In 1990, five-year plans were abandoned in favor of the free market, bilateral trade agreements, and convertible curren-cies. The organization formally voted to rename itself the Organization for International Economic Cooperation in 1991. The organization still exists, but is of very limited influence.

Places and Things
Building Alliances, Combating Communism, and Fostering Recovery

ATLANTIC CHARTER (1941)

Between August 9 and 12, 1941, U.S. President Franklin D. Roosevelt and British Prime Minister Winston Churchill held a series of secret meetings aboard two ships anchored off the coast of Newfoundland. Great Britain was at war with Germany at the time, fighting a desperate battle to prevent Germany's complete victory in World War II. The U.S. had not yet entered the war (that would come in December of the same year). The resulting agreement between the United States and Britain was called the Atlantic Charter and was announced to the world on 14 August. Although it was neither an alliance nor a binding legal commitment, the agreement articulated the shared goals of the United Kingdom and the United States to end territorial aggression and war around the world. By the end of the following month, fifteen other countries, all opposed to Nazi Germany, had signed the Atlantic Charter as well. The document cleared the way for the later formation of the Allied Powers to fight the Germans and their Japanese and Italian allies when the United States entered World War II.

EASTERN EUROPE

The concept of Eastern Europe commonly includes most, if not all, European countries that were Communist states or under Soviet control until the end of the Cold War. Increasingly, Eastern Europe is defined today in a more geographical manner, with the region comprising the area between Central Europe and Russia.

FOUR POINT PLAN (1949)

President Harry Truman stated four major U.S. foreign policy goals, known as the Four Point Plan, during his inaugural address on January 20, 1949: (1) the continued support for the United Nations; (2) the continuation of programs for world economic recovery;

Places and Things
Building Alliances, Combating Communism, and Fostering Recovery, cont.

(3) the establishment of agreements among "freedom-loving nations" to protect against the "dangers of aggression"; and (4) the launch of a "bold new program" that would make the benefits of American scientific advances and industrial progress available for the improvement and growth of underdeveloped regions.

GEORGE F. KENNAN'S CONTAINMENT DOCTRINE (1947)

In July, 1947, U.S. ambassador to the Soviet Union George F. Kennan published an article in the journal *Foreign Affairs* and signed it simply "X." The essay articulated his policy of containing Communism where it already existed at that time and actively preventing its spread to other countries. Although the article was published anonymously, Kennan's authorship was quickly established. Dubbed the "Containment Doctrine," this policy was enthusiastically embraced by President Harry Truman and became the foundation during the Cold War years.

MOLOTOV PLAN (1947)

The Molotov Plan, proposed by Foreign Minister Vyacheslav Molotov, was adopted by the Soviet Union to create an economic union of Eastern European countries. The intent was to rebuild the countries' postwar economies according to a strategy set forth by the Communist Parties of each participating nation. The nations involved in the Molotov Plan were the Soviet Union, Poland, East Germany, Czechoslovakia, Bulgaria, Hungary, and Romania.

MUTUAL SECURITY ACT (1951)

In an effort to extend the Marshall Plan, the U.S. Congress passed the Mutual Security Act on October 31, 1951. The act distributed $7 billion in foreign aid and created the Mutual Security Agency.

TRUMAN DOCTRINE (1947)

On March 12, 1947, in a message to the U.S. Congress, U.S. President Harry Truman laid out a foreign policy doctrine for the United States in the early days of the Cold War that subsequently became known as the Truman Doctrine. At heart, the policy was one that mandated an active role for the United States in containing the spread of Communism around the world. In particular, Truman spoke in reference to Greece and Turkey, both of which were in need of significant economic aid to stave off Communist revolutions. He believed that the Soviet Union was directly funding Communist forces within the two countries and felt the United States should support the anti-Communists. The aid Truman envisaged was primarily financial, which Congress granted by appropriating $400 million to the two countries. The Truman Doctrine laid the groundwork for the Marshall Plan, which extended similar aid to all of Western Europe. It also formed the backbone of America's Cold War policy and led to both financial and military entanglements throughout the world, including the Korean War and the Vietnam War.

WESTERN EUROPE

Basically composed of the victorious European countries of World War II, Western Europe is primarily a political concept that sprang from postwar conditions and became rooted in the Cold War. Western Europe was the bloc of nations that, with the U.S., served as a counter-weight to the Soviet Union and Eastern Europe. In addition to geographical differences, Western Europe can also be distinguished from Eastern Europe by economics and culture. Western Europe is commonly associated with liberal Democracy and Capitalism, and most of the countries share some historical connections with the United States and Canada.

Events and Eras
Building Alliances, Combating Communism, and Fostering Recovery

COLD WAR (1945–1989)

"Let us not be deceived—today we are in the midst of a cold war." Thus spoke Bernard Baruch, a wealthy financier and presidential adviser, in a speech in April, 1947. He had coined the term that would come to define the monumental struggle between the United States and its allies and the Soviet Union and its partners that began shortly after the end of World War II and continued until the dissolution of the Soviet Union in 1989. Based on fundamental ideological differences, a deep-seated distrust of each other, and an escalating arms race, the Cold War shaped the international world order for more than forty years and profoundly influenced the politics and economies of many nations.

The arms race fueled by the Cold War was expensive and dangerous—costing both the United States and the Soviet Union billions of dollars, and bringing questionable security at best. Many peace advocates thought that the arms buildup was a greater threat to the United States than the Soviets were and advocated bilateral or even unilateral arms reductions in an effort to diminish the ever-growing threat of nuclear war.

This threat became frighteningly real in 1962, when the Soviets attempted to put missiles in Cuba. Following a short standoff, during which President John F. Kennedy threatened nuclear retaliation, the Soviets agreed to withdraw their missiles in return for Kennedy's promise not to invade Cuba. Both nations were sufficiently frightened by this episode that they began a period of de-escalation, commonly called *détente*. This period lasted from 1963 to 1980, when the Soviets invaded Afghanistan and the United States elected Ronald Reagan president. These events reignited the arms race and the Cold War until 1985, when Mikhail Gorbachev came to power in the Soviet Union. Gorbachev sought to ease tensions with the West while relaxing internal controls within the Soviet system. Within four years, Gorbachev's policies of *glasnost* ("openness") and *perestroika* ("restructuring") led to the downfall of Communism, first in the Soviet satellite nations, and then in the Soviet Union itself, which was dissolved into many independent states. Although most observers consider the dissolution of the U.S.S.R. to mark the end of the Cold War, both the United States and Russia (as well as several other former Soviet states) maintain significant nuclear arsenals. Although the tensions of the Cold War are significantly reduced, the threat of nuclear war has not disappeared.

BERLIN BLOCKADE (1948–1949)

The Berlin blockade was the first serious crisis of the Cold War. The Soviet Union imposed the blockade in an attempt to limit the ability of the United States, Great Britain, and France to travel to their sector of Berlin, which lay within Soviet-occupied East Germany.

As a result of the Potsdam Agreement in 1945, Germany and Berlin were divided into occupation zones by the Allies (United States, Soviet Union, France, and Great Britain), reaffirming principles laid out earlier at the Yalta Conference. Although the provisions of the agreement allocated occupation sectors of the city for the other three Allies, there were no arrangements for access to Berlin through the Soviet zone.

After the war, the relationship between the Soviet Union and the West began to deteriorate steadily. In late 1947, discussions about Germany broke down over Soviet charges that the other former Allied powers were violating the Potsdam Agreement. On March 20, 1948, the Soviets withdrew from the Four Power Allied

Events and Eras
Building Alliances, Combating Communism, and Fostering Recovery, cont.

Control Council administering Berlin. Ten days later, guards on the East German border began slowing the entry of Western troop trains bound for Berlin. On June 7, the Western powers announced their intention to proceed with the creation of West Germany. On June 15, the Soviets declared the autobahn entering Berlin from West Germany "closed for repairs." Three days later, all road traffic was stopped crossing the sector boundaries and on June 21, barge traffic was prohibited from entering the city. On June 24, the Soviets stopped all surface traffic between West Germany and Berlin, arguing that if Germany was to be partitioned, Berlin could no longer be the single German capital.

Located 110 miles inside the Soviet occupation zone, West Berlin from the start of the Cold War was a Western outpost deep within the Communist bloc, a hotbed of intelligence operations for both sides, and the best available escape route for East Germans fleeing Communist and Soviet control. U.S. president Harry Truman was convinced that losing Berlin would mean losing all of Germany. He believed the Soviets were determined to push the Western powers out of Berlin, and thereby discredit the value of U.S. assurances to its allies and the rest of Europe.

After a military response was considered and rejected, the Western powers, foremost among them the United States, undertook to supply West Berlin through air corridors left open to them in a postwar agreement in what became known as the Berlin Airlift. Beginning on June 24, 1948 and continuing for the next 324 days, Western pilots made 272,000 flights into West Berlin, delivering thousands of tons of supplies every day. At the height of the operation on April 16, 1949, an Allied aircraft landed in Berlin every minute. The airlift was an international effort; the airplanes were supplied by the United States, Great Britain, and France, but there were also flight crews from Australia, Canada, South Africa, and New Zealand. At first, the airlift was meant to be a short-term measure because the Allied officials did not believe that the airlift could support the whole of Berlin for any length of time. The situation in the summer and fall of 1948 was very tense as the Soviets buzzed U.S. transport planes in the air corridors over East Germany, but the Allies only increased their efforts to resupply the German city once it became apparent that no resolution was in sight.

The effort gained wide public sympathy. On May 12, 1949 the Soviets, concluding that the blockade had failed, reopened the borders in return for scheduling a meeting of the Council of Foreign Ministers, perhaps believing that they could have some influence on the Western Allies' proposed plans for the future of Germany. Even though the Soviets lifted the blockade, the airlift did not end until September 30 because the Western nations wanted to build up sufficient amounts of reserve supplies in West Berlin in case the Soviets blockaded it again.

In the end, the blockade turned out to be ineffective, and it backfired on the Soviets in several ways. It provoked genuine fears of the Soviets in the West and added increased impetus to the Cold War. Instead of preventing the establishment of an independent West Germany, it accelerated the Allies' plans to set up the state. It also hastened the creation of the North Atlantic Treaty Organization (NATO), a U.S.–Western European military alliance.

Background
Building Alliances, Combating Communism, and Fostering Recovery

MARSHALL PLAN (1947)

The Marshall Plan was the comprehensive project designed and implemented by the Truman administration to underwrite restoration of Western Europe's World War II-ravaged economy.

The Marshall Plan to aid in rebuilding Europe after World War II was proposed in 1947 and signed into law in 1948 during the administration of President Harry S Truman. The Economic Cooperation Administration (ECA) administered the plan, which also was known as the European Recovery Plan (ERP). The plan was designed to enhance America's long-term economic, political, and strategic interests at a time when Western European economies faced devastation following the end of World War II. The Marshall Plan was to accomplish this in three ways. First, U.S. policy makers believed that recovered Western European economies could provide a desired market for American goods and help make the United States a leading economic power in the postwar world. Second, they envisioned Western Europe as part of a multilateral system of world trade crucial to the liberal capitalist economy that Washington had in mind for itself and its allies. Unity in Western Europe would foster an American-type liberal capitalist order able to create high productivity, comfortable living standards, and political stability. Third, the U.S. government saw the Marshall Plan as a means of strengthening shaky pro-American governments in Western European nations and a way of warding off rapid inroads being made by domestic Communist parties and left-wing organizations leaning toward the Soviet Union. Thus, the European Recovery Plan was an all-embracing effort for the economic revival of Western Europe as a whole that would capitalize upon that economic strength to accomplish definite political goals for the United States.

U.S. Secretary of State George Marshall first publicized such a plan in a commencement speech at Harvard University on June 5, 1947. To avoid the Marshall Plan being viewed as anti-Soviet, Marshall subsequently invited the Soviet Union and its Eastern European satellite states to participate in its design; all the while, U.S. policymakers anticipated a rejection from Moscow. The Soviet Union, together with Poland and Czechoslovakia, appeared at the first planning conference (convened in Paris on June 27, 1947) for Marshall's proposal, but as the United States had predicted, the Soviets quickly withdrew, denouncing the plan as an attempt to build an anti-Soviet bloc of Western capitalist powers. Lengthy negotiations followed without the Soviets; participants (seventeen Western European nations in all) laid the groundwork for a four-year recovery plan. On the plan's completion, the United States created the Economic Cooperation Administration (ECA). The Organization for European Economic Cooperation (OEEC) established by the seventeen Western European states would coordinate the American effort.

From 1948 to 1952, $13.15 billion in Marshall Plan aid helped revitalize Western Europe and ushered it onto a path of durable economic growth and integration. The recharged economies that owed their lives to the Marshall Plan led to more stable political systems that discouraged Communist encroachment in Western Europe. In addition, the United States buttressed its economic and political influence over Western Europe. Finally, the Marshall Plan widened the Cold War gulf between the United States and the Soviet Union. Rather than surrender Communism and its command economy to an American-dominated Capitalist system, The Soviet Union began its draconian policy of quarantining its Eastern European client states from the rest of Europe.

World
Leadership
and Unclear
Mission

Defining Moment

National Archives

Associated Press

World Leadership and Unclear Mission

Marking one of the most traumatic periods of U.S. history, the Vietnam War caused massive disruption in Southeast Asia. Although U.S. leaders were often torn about American involvement in Vietnam, many modern observers view the Vietnam War as a failed attempt at nation-building by the United States.

After France's devastating loss to Vietnamese Communist insurgents at the Battle of Dien Bien Phu in May, 1954 ended almost a century of French control of Vietnam, the United States elected to assume responsibility for South Vietnam. That decision was guided by the U.S. government's so-called containment policy, which strongly advocated preventing the spread of Communism during the Cold War by aiding countries fighting against Communist forces.

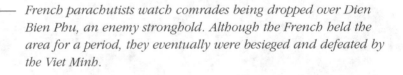

French parachutists watch comrades being dropped over Dien Bien Phu, an enemy stronghold. Although the French held the area for a period, they eventually were besieged and defeated by the Viet Minh.

Hulton Archive/Getty Images

A few months after the Geneva Conference of 1954 officially ended the Indochina War, the United States orchestrated a collective security arrangement for Southeast Asia known as the Southeast Asia Treaty Organization (SEATO). When SEATO failed to establish an effective defensive arrangement for Southeast Asia, U.S. president Dwight D. Eisenhower abandoned the allied approach in the spring of 1955 and moved in a unilateral direction, dedicating the United States to building a strong democratic Vietnamese nation in the South under the leadership of the enigmatic Ngo Dinh Diem.

Diem faced enormous challenges in governing South Vietnam, not least because the small cadres of Vietnamese insurgents left behind in the South, known as Viet Cong, still advocated for the adoption of

Communism in the country. He also faced several other civil insurrections of groups opposed to his rule, and charges of corruption plagued his government. Despite sometimes tense relations with the United States, he managed to retain U.S. support for his shaky regime.

U.S. president Dwight D. Eisenhower welcomes the president of the Republic of Vietnam, Ngo Dinh Diem, at Washington National Airport in 1957. Under Eisenhower, the United States created the Military Assistance Advisory Group (MAAG) for Indochina, channeling money and, later, military advisers to Vietnam. American interest in preventing Communism from spreading to Asia through political and financial influence led to several conflicts, including the Vietnam War.

National Archives

U.S. leaders never persuaded Diem to undertake the reforms needed to win support for his government from the Vietnamese people nor to address seriously the corruption that engulfed the country. Diem, in turn, increasingly came to fear the escalating American presence as much as he feared his internal enemies. His concerns were not completely unwarranted. With his advisers greatly divided over what to do about Diem, U.S. president John F. Kennedy tacitly agreed to a coup by South Vietnamese generals in November, 1963, although Kennedy was shocked by Diem's murder during the takeover.

After Kennedy was assassinated only three weeks after Diem's ouster, Lyndon B. Johnson continued his predecessor's policies in Vietnam, then escalated U.S. involvement. In March, 1965, Johnson authorized a series of retaliatory air strikes against the Communist North Vietnamese that continued nearly unabated for more than three years. In addition, U.S. general William C. Westmoreland, with more than 500,000 troops at his disposal, implemented a strategy of attrition and "search-and-destroy" tactics.

Under Johnson, the United States continued its attempt to use economic and military aid to create a stable, democratic government in South Vietnam. A series of short-lived military regimes held power until June, 1965, until some stability was restored by the National Leadership

World Leadership
and Unclear Mission, cont.

Committee with Lieutenant General Nguyen Van Thieu as its chairperson. In 1967, Thieu was elected president, bringing renewed hope in the United States that democracy had taken root in South Vietnam.

With President Johnson standing at his side, South Vietnamese president Nguyen Van Thieu speaks to the crowd after his arrival at Hickham Air Force Base, Honolulu, Hawaii, on July 19, 1968.

Thieu proved to be a canny political operator, but he was unable to overcome an abysmal lack of public support, massive government corruption, and the burgeoning Communist insurgency. He never established a firm base of political support, nor did he find any way to address public demands for political, social, or economic reform. Instead, his repressive rule and the outright thievery by his officials alienated large portions of the population and laid the groundwork for an eventual Communist victory.

Back in the United States, President Richard Nixon responded in 1969 to growing public sentiment against the war by instituting the gradual withdrawal of U.S. troops and replacing them with South Vietnamese forces, a policy known as "Vietnamization." Over the next few years, the South Vietnamese troops proved to be no match for their North Vietnamese counterparts. After the Paris Peace Accord (1973) ended direct U.S. combat involvement in the Vietnam War, there was no stopping North Vietnam from achieving victory. By early 1975, the North Vietnamese forces had penetrated deep into South Vietnam, reaching the capital city of Saigon and prompting the South Vietnamese government to surrender on April 30, 1975. The previous day, television screens in the United States had displayed footage of Americans being evacuated by helicopter from the roof of the U.S. Embassy in Saigon, providing dramatic evidence that the U.S. government's efforts at nation-building in Vietnam had failed.

Lesson Overview

This activity should let students explore the issues surrounding the Vietnam War. They will need a general background in the issues of the Cold War, American attitudes toward it, and how both were played out in Asia in the 1950s and 1960s. The activity is divided into three parts.

In Part I, students will learn about the role of political rhetoric in the decision to go to war in Vietnam by analyzing the themes of a speech by President Johnson in the opening days of the conflict and completing a short writing assignment.

In Part II, the students will study the role of the media in creating public perception of U.S. activities in Vietnam by viewing a series of photographs.

In Part III, the students will take what they have learned and write an analysis of the failure of U.S. nation-building in Vietnam.

World Leadership and Unclear Mission

Authors

CHRIS MULLIN
SANTA YNEZ VALLEY
UNION HIGH SCHOOL

BRETT PIERSMA
SANTA YNEZ VALLEY
UNION HIGH SCHOOL

Lesson Plan Part I
Found Poetry

The teacher will begin by dividing the students into twelve groups, each one ideally containing two to three students. To each group, the teacher will give one of Excerpts 1–12 of President Lyndon Johnson's 1965 speech at Johns Hopkins University.

The teacher will ask each group to select a reporter who will read aloud the provided excerpt to that team alone. Once the reporters have read aloud their documents, each group should discuss and clarify the meaning of the primary source.

Now that the teams have completed their first read-through, the reporter will read the short passage a second time. At this time, the teacher should direct the students to actively listen for words and key phrases that stand out and write them down.

Once each group has heard its passage read aloud twice, each student in the group will use it to each complete a *found poem.* A found poem can take on a variety of forms. The most essential component of a found poem is that it uses words or phrases that someone else has already spoken or written. The job of the students is to simply weave the words of others into a poetic form. The students are free to add their own words as well as to repeat key phrases for emphasis. The found poems do not need to rhyme. The teacher should require that the poems be at least fifty words long and suggest using the words and key phrases that the student wrote down.

Once every student in the class has written a short poem, the teacher will ask the members of the small teams to share their work aloud with each other. The teacher will ask each team to select whichever poem they felt was the best.

Activity
LESSON PLAN PART I

For this portion of the activity, students will need copies of:

PRIMARY SOURCES
• Excerpts 1–12:
  President Johnson's 1965
  Speech, pp. 111–122

Now that each team has selected its favorite poem, the teacher will have each group present it to the full class. The teacher should have the class present their poems in the order of their documents; for example, the small group that had Johnson speech Excerpt 1 will read first. The team that had Johnson speech Excerpt 12 will read last.

Once the class has heard all the short found poems, the teacher should lead the class in a discussion using the following guided questions:

- To what part of the world is President Johnson's speech referring?
- What seems to be going on in that part of the world?
- What is life like for the people living there?
- What challenges are they facing?
- What does President Johnson recommend that the United States do?

Lesson Plan Part II
Photo Journalist

The teacher will now tell the students that they are going to be American newspaper reporters traveling through Vietnam. Ahead of time, the teacher should have placed Photos 1–9 around the room. (The teacher should laminate these images if possible.) The students should walk around the room with pen and paper and look at as many photos as they can in five-to-ten minutes.

Now that the students have had a chance to look at snapshots of events in Vietnam, the teacher will ask students to focus on just one picture and write 100 words about it as if they were an American newspaper reporter writing back home to their papers. The teacher should require that the students try to integrate their understanding of President Johnson's 1965 speech into their news articles. The students may want to focus on the following questions:

- What is happening in the picture?
- How does this event relate to President Johnson's message?
- Is the United States helping to fulfill its promise?
- What roles are the Vietnamese people playing?
- Do the Vietnamese people depicted seem happy with the American involvement?
- Do you think this is evidence of a positive or negative American influence in Vietnam?
- Do you think America should keep up its nation-building effort in the region?

Activity
LESSON PLAN PART II

For this portion of the activity, you will need copies of:

PRIMARY SOURCES
- Photos 1–9, pp. 123–131
- Photos 10–18, pp. 132–140 (copied separately or on the backs of Photos 1–9)

The teacher will now tell the students that they are once again going to be American newspaper reporters. This time, however, the teacher will have quietly turned around the first nine pictures hanging around the room, now exposing Photos 10–18. The students should once again walk around the room and look at the pictures for five-to-ten minutes.

Once the students have had a chance to investigate the new photos, the teacher will again ask them to focus on just one picture and write 100 words about it. The images of events in these pictures are quite different, but the teacher should require that the students again try to integrate their understanding of President Johnson's 1965 speech into their news articles. The students may want to focus on the following questions:

- What is happening in the picture?
- How does this event relate to President Johnson's initial message?
- What roles are the Vietnamese people playing (if applicable to your picture)?
- What roles are the American people playing (if applicable to your picture)?
- What role is the U.S. army playing?
- Do you think the U.S. effort in Vietnam should be continued?

Lesson Plan Part III
Final Extension Writing

This series of activities has deliberately left out a central piece to the Vietnam puzzle. Students began the unit by looking at the 1965 nation-building proposals of President Johnson as well as at a series of photographs that seemed to confirm that America was successful in doing much more than merely conducting a literal war against Communism. Later, however, students looked at a series of images that revealed a downside to the American involvement in Vietnam and fierce popular opposition to American intervention, both in Vietnam and back home in the United States. In this final activity, students will be asked to use their research and analytical skills to answer the simple question:

WHAT WENT WRONG?

In answering this question, students may consider some of the following points: Why did the Marshall plan, dedicated to the same principles as the Johnson administration, flourish so resoundingly in Europe while the American goals for Vietnam ended in disaster and defeat? What was different about Vietnam? What did America do wrong? What did the Johnson Administration not understand? What could our nation have done differently to provide Vietnam with the prosperity, liberty, and security promised by President Lyndon Johnson at Johns Hopkins University in 1965?

Students should be encouraged to use the Internet, textbooks, and the library to form well-written answers to this question.

Primary Sources

World
Leadership and
Unclear Mission

President Lyndon B. Johnson as he speaks to an audience at Johns Hopkins University in 1965. With American involvement in the Vietnam conflict accelerating, Johnson sought to justify American intervention by speaking of the nation's history of fighting for freedom and her duty to protect the world from Communism.

Time Life Pictures/Getty Images

Excerpt 1
Johnson Speech

Tonight Americans and Asians are dying for a world where each people may choose its own path to change. This is the principle for which our ancestors fought in the valleys of Pennsylvania. It is the principle for which our sons fight tonight in the jungles of Viet-Nam. Viet-Nam is far away from this quiet campus. We have no territory there, nor do we seek any. The war is dirty and brutal and difficult. And some 400 young men, born into an America that is bursting with opportunity and promise, have ended their lives on Viet-Nam's steaming soil. Why must we take this painful road? Why must this Nation hazard its ease, and its interest, and its power for the sake of a people so far away? We fight because we must fight if we are to live in a world where every country can shape its own destiny. And only in such a world will our own freedom be finally secure. This kind of world will never be built by bombs or bullets. Yet the infirmities of man are such that force must often precede reason, and the waste of war, the works of peace. We wish that this were not so. But we must deal with the world as it is, if it is ever to be as we wish.

Excerpt 2
Johnson Speech

The world as it is in Asia is not a serene or peaceful place. The first reality is that North Viet-Nam has attacked the independent nation of South Viet-Nam. Its object is total conquest. Of course, some of the people of South Viet-Nam are participating in the attack on their own government. But trained men and supplies, orders and arms, flow in a constant stream from north to south. This support is the heartbeat of the war. And it is a war of unparalleled brutality. Simple farmers are the targets of assassination and kidnapping. Women and children are strangled in the night because their men are loyal to their government. And helpless villages are ravaged by sneak attacks. Large-scale raids are conducted on towns, and terror strikes in the heart of cities. The confused nature of this conflict cannot mask the fact that it is the new face of an old enemy. Over this war—and all Asia—is another reality: the deepening shadow of Communist China. The rulers in Hanoi are urged on by Peking. This is a regime which has destroyed freedom in Tibet, which has attacked India, and has been condemned by the United Nations for aggression in Korea. It is a nation which is helping the forces of violence in almost every continent. The contest in Viet-Nam is part of a wider pattern of aggressive purposes.

Excerpt 3
Johnson Speech

Why are we in South Viet-Nam? We are there because we have a promise to keep. Since 1954 every American President has offered support to the people of South Viet-Nam. We have helped to build, and we have helped to defend. Thus, over many years, we have made a national pledge to help South Viet-Nam defend its independence. And I intend to keep that promise. To dishonor that pledge, to abandon this small and brave nation to its enemies, and to the terror that must follow, would be an unforgivable wrong. We are also there to strengthen world order. Around the globe, from Berlin to Thailand, are people whose well-being rests, in part, on the belief that they can count on us if they are attacked. To leave Viet-Nam to its fate would shake the confidence of all these people in the value of an American commitment and in the value of America's word. The result would be increased unrest and instability, and even wider war. We are also there because there are great stakes in the balance. Let no one think for a moment that retreat from Viet-Nam would bring an end to conflict. The battle would be renewed in one country and then another.

Excerpt 4
Johnson Speech

The central lesson of our time is that the appetite of aggression is never satisfied. To withdraw from one battlefield means only to prepare for the next. We must say in southeast Asia—as we did in Europe—in the words of the Bible: *"Hitherto shalt thou come, but no further."* There are those who say that all our effort there will be futile—that China's power is such that it is bound to dominate all southeast Asia. But there is no end to that argument until all of the nations of Asia are swallowed up. There are those who wonder why we have a responsibility there. Well, we have it there for the same reason that we have a responsibility for the defense of Europe. World War II was fought in both Europe and Asia, and when it ended we found ourselves with continued responsibility for the defense of freedom.

Excerpt 5
Johnson Speech

Our objective is the independence of South Viet-Nam, and its freedom from attack. We want nothing for ourselves—only that the people of South Viet-Nam be allowed to guide their own country in their own way. We will do everything necessary to reach that objective. And we will do only what is absolutely necessary . . . We hope that peace will come swiftly. But that is in the hands of others besides ourselves. And we must be prepared for a long continued conflict. It will require patience as well as bravery, the will to endure as well as the will to resist. I wish it were possible to convince others with words of what we now find it necessary to say with guns and planes: armed hostility is futile. Our resources are equal to any challenge. Because we fight for values and we fight for principles, rather than territory or colonies, our patience and our determination are unending. Once this is clear, then it should also be clear that the only path for reasonable men is the path of peaceful settlement.

Excerpt 6
Johnson Speech

We have no desire to see thousands die in battle—Asians or Americans. We have no desire to devastate that which the people of North Viet-Nam have built with toil and sacrifice. We will use our power with restraint and with all the wisdom that we can command. But we will use it. This war, like most wars, is filled with terrible irony. For what do the people of North Viet-Nam want? They want what their neighbors also desire: food for their hunger; health for their bodies; a chance to learn; progress for their country; and an end to the bondage of material misery. And they would find all these things far more readily in peaceful association with others than in the endless course of battle.

Excerpt 7
Johnson Speech

These countries of southeast Asia are homes for millions of impover-
ished people. Each day these people rise at dawn and struggle through
until the night to wrestle existence from the soil. They are often
wracked by disease, plagued by hunger, and death comes at the early
age of 40. Stability and peace do not come easily in such a land.
Neither independence nor human dignity will ever be won, though, by
arms alone. It also requires the work of peace. The American people
have helped generously in times past in these works. Now there must
be a much more massive effort to improve the life of man in that
conflict-torn corner of our world . . . For our part I will ask the
Congress to join in a billion dollar American investment in this effort as
soon as it is underway. And I would hope that all other industrialized
countries, including the Soviet Union, will join in this effort to replace
despair with hope, and terror with progress.

Excerpt 8
Johnson Speech

The task is nothing less than to enrich the hopes and the existence of more than a hundred million people. And there is much to be done. The vast Mekong River can provide food and water and power on a scale to dwarf even our own TVA. The wonders of modern medicine can be spread through villages where thousands die every year from lack of care. Schools can be established to train people in the skills that are needed to manage the process of development . . . I also intend to expand and speed up a program to make available our farm surpluses to assist in feeding and clothing the needy in Asia. We should not allow people to go hungry and wear rags while our own warehouses overflow with an abundance of wheat and corn, rice and cotton . . . In areas that are still ripped by conflict, of course development will not be easy. Peace will be necessary for final success. But we cannot and must not wait for peace to begin this job.

Excerpt 9
Johnson Speech

This will be a disorderly planet for a long time. In Asia, as elsewhere, the forces of the modern world are shaking old ways and uprooting ancient civilizations. There will be turbulence and struggle and even violence. Great social change—as we see in our own country now—does not always come without conflict. We must also expect that nations will on occasion be in dispute with us. It may be because we are rich, or powerful; or because we have made some mistakes; or because they honestly fear our intentions. However, no nation need ever fear that we desire their land, or to impose our will, or to dictate their institutions. But we will always oppose the effort of one nation to conquer another nation. We will do this because our own security is at stake. But there is more to it than that. For our generation has a dream. It is a very old dream. But we have the power and now we have the opportunity to make that dream come true. For centuries nations have struggled among each other. But we dream of a world where disputes are settled by law and reason. And we will try to make it so.

Excerpt 10
Johnson Speech

For most of history men have hated and killed one another in battle. But we dream of an end to war. And we will try to make it so. For all existence most men have lived in poverty, threatened by hunger. But we dream of a world where all are fed and charged with hope. And we will help to make it so. The ordinary men and women of North Viet-Nam and South Viet-Nam—of China and India—of Russia and America—are brave people. They are filled with the same proportions of hate and fear, of love and hope. Most of them want the same things for themselves and their families. Most of them do not want their sons to ever die in battle, or to see their homes, or the homes of others, destroyed. Well, this can be their world yet. Man now has the knowledge—always before denied—to make this planet serve the real needs of the people who live on it. I know this will not be easy. I know how difficult it is for reason to guide passion, and love to master hate. The complexities of this world do not bow easily to pure and consistent answers. But the simple truths are there just the same. We must all try to follow them as best we can.

Excerpt 11
Johnson Speech

We often say how impressive power is. But I do not find it impressive at all. The guns and the bombs, the rockets and the warships, are all symbols of human failure. They are necessary symbols. They protect what we cherish. But they are witness to human folly. A dam built across a great river is impressive. In the countryside where I was born, and where I live, I have seen the night illuminated, and the kitchens warmed, and the homes heated, where once the cheerless night and the ceaseless cold held sway. And all this happened because electricity came to our area along the humming wires of the REA. Electrification of the country-side—yes, that, too, is impressive. A rich harvest in a hungry land is impressive. The sight of healthy children in a classroom is impressive. These—not mighty arms—are the achievements which the American Nation believes to be impressive. And, if we are steadfast, the time may come when all other nations will also find it so.

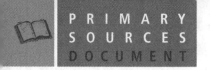
Excerpt 12
Johnson Speech

Every night before I turn out the lights to sleep I ask myself this question: Have I done everything that I can do to unite this country? Have I done everything I can to help unite the world, to try to bring peace and hope to all the peoples of the world? Have I done enough? Ask yourselves that question in your homes—and in this hall tonight. Have we, each of us, all done all we could? Have we done enough? . . . This generation of the world must choose: destroy or build, kill or aid, hate or understand. We can do all these things on a scale never dreamed of before. Well, we will choose life. In so doing we will prevail over the enemies within man, and over the natural enemies of all mankind.

Photo 1

The 'Other War' in Vietnam

TO KEEP A VILLAGE FREE

After a fishing trip, a Marine and his young friend return to Hoa Hiep

AUGUST 25 · 1967 · 35¢

Time Life Pictures/Getty Images

Cover of *Life* magazine August 25, 1967 entitled "The 'Other War' in Vietnam: to Keep a Village Free." The photo, features an American soldier and an injured Vietnamese boy.

Photo 2

National Archives

Children gather before the new market in Tinh Thuong, which was built with assistance by the government of Vietnam and the U.S. Agency for International Development (USAID). USAID was the agency responsible for providing economic aid for programs in South Vietnam.

Photo 3

Time Life Pictures/Getty Images

U.S. Marines in Vietnam
line a village well
with cement.

Photo 4

Corbis/Bettmann

A U.S. soldier and a
Vietnamese child ride the
swings in a relaxed and
happy moment.

Photo 5

Associated Press

A Navy medical corpsman
treats a child at Nguoi
Trong in August, 1966,
during the Vietnam War.

Photo 6

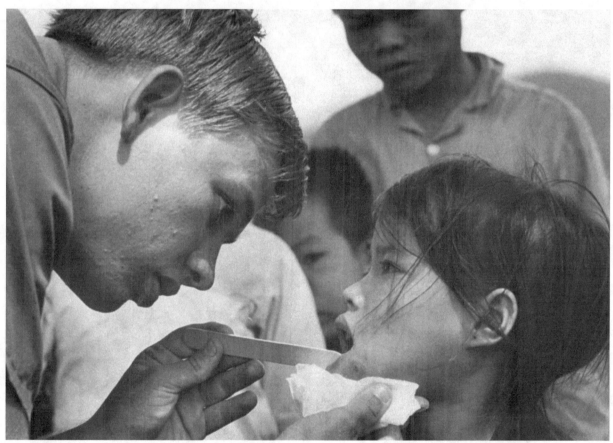

Time Life Pictures/Getty Images

A U.S. Navy corpsman examines a girl in the village of Hao Hiep. The American military brought some valuable services to Vietnam that included healthcare.

Photo 7

Time Life Pictures/Getty Images

Dr. William E. Owen

playing with

Vietnamese children.

Photo 8

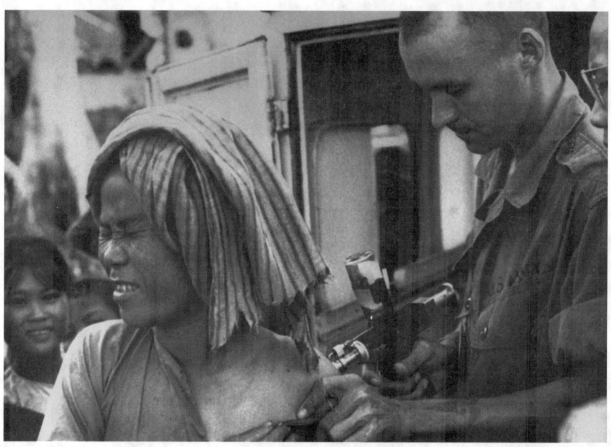

Time Life Pictures/Getty Images

U.S. Navy corpsman inoculates a flood refugee on Nui Sam mountain. American troops were often drawn into daily affairs in Vietnam and tried to help when they could.

Photo 9

National Archives

Marine Staff Sergeant
Ermalinda Salazar volunteers to
help children at the St. Vincent
de Paul Orphanage in Vietnam.
American troops were often
moved by the sufferings exacer-
bated by the war in Vietnam.

Photo 10

Associated Press

Buddhist monks and women pull
at a barbed wire road barricade
at a Buddhist demonstration in
Saigon on July 17, 1963. The
Buddhists were protesting the
policies of South Vietnamese
President Ngo Dinh Diem, who
was Roman Catholic.

Photo 11

Associated Press

Buddhist monk Quang Duc burns himself to death on a Saigon street June 11, 1963 to protest alleged persecution of Buddhists by the South Vietnamese government.

Photo 12

President Lyndon
B. Johnson listens
to a tape sent by
Captain Charles
Robb from Vietnam,
on July 31, 1968.

National Archives

Photo 13

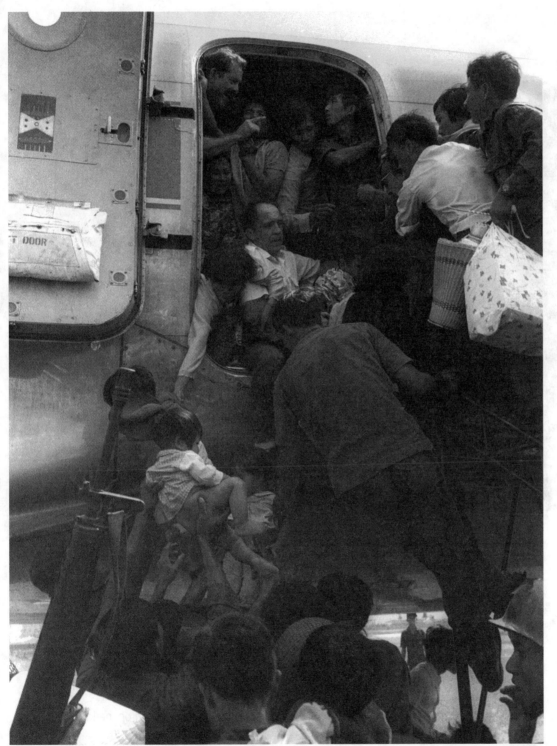

Associated Press

A U.S. civilian pilot tries to maintain order as South Vietnamese civilians scramble to get aboard during evacuation of Nha Trang as North Vietnamese forces approach the city on April 1, 1975.

Photo 14

Time Life Pictures/Getty Images

Mary Ann Vecchio kneels over
student Jeffrey Miller, killed during
an anti-war demonstration at Kent
State University, Ohio, May 4, 1970.
Three other students also died when
National Guardsmen opened fire on
a campus anti-war protest.

Photo 15

Associated Press

South Vietnamese
National Police Chief
Brigadier General
Nguyen Ngoc Loan
summarily executes an
enemy guerrilla on
February 1, 1968.

Photo 16

Corbis-Bettmann

Young pacifists burn their
draft cards in Boston on
March 31, 1966.

Photo 17

Associated Press

U.S. Marshals drag away an anti-war protester after he attempted to break through the security lines at the Pentagon in Washington, D.C. on October 21, 1967. Mass anti-war protests were common in the United States during the 1960s, especially among the younger generation.

Photo 18

Library of Congress

Demonstrators protest the trial of the Chicago Seven (also known as the Chicago Eight). The defendants were anti-war activists arrested for conspiring to incite riots during the 1968 Democratic National Convention in Chicago.

Glossary Words, Ideas, or Movements
World Leadership and Unclear Mission

COMMUNISM A social system in which a classless society owns and shares all property as a whole.

CONTAINMENT A policy first implemented by the United States in 1947 in response to communism. It is meant to prevent—through political, economic, and diplomatic methods—the growth of a hostile country's territory and to limit the country's ideological influence.

DOMINO THEORY The view held by U.S. policy makers during the Cold War that if one country fell to Communism, its neighbors were threatened with a chain reaction of Communist takeovers. First publicly expressed by President Dwight D. Eisenhower at a press conference in 1954, the domino theory arose from fear that the withdrawal of colonial powers from Southeast Asia would lead to the fall of Vietnam, then the rest of Southeast Asia, and perhaps India, Japan, the Philippines, and Indonesia.

FOREIGN POLICY A country's goals in relation to other nations and the methods and strategies used to achieve them, including diplomacy, technical assistance, and economic aid.

GUERRILLA WARFARE Spanish term for "little war" that came into common usage at the time the Spanish came into conflict with Napoléon I's forces in the first decade of the 19th century. Although guerrilla war may have obtained its name in that conflict, its concept and practice date back many centuries, and it is probably impossible to find a record of its first use.

Glossary Words, Ideas, or Movements
World Leadership and Unclear Mission, cont.

Guerrilla warfare is basically the harassing of a superior force by an inferior one. The key to guerrilla warfare—especially in its beginning stages—is to avoid direct contact with the stronger enemy at all costs. Thus, guerrillas attack isolated outposts and units with quick assaults and temporarily superior numbers, and then fade into the countryside before a response can be mounted. The ultimate goal of guerrilla fighting is usually to gain enough numbers to be able to switch to a more conventional warfare fighting between large armies. At that point, the guerrilla forces may actually win the conflict and implement their own policies, be they political, religious, social, or any combination of these.

INSURGENCY A revolt against an established government not reaching the proportions of a full-scale revolution. Though an insurgency is generally recognized as a domestic matter by the international community, if it persists it may become a civil war and the insurgents may be recognized as "belligerents," making them subject to scrutiny by the international community.

NATION-BUILDING The process of rebuilding a nation's economic, social, and political institutions to establish the armed forces, police, government, banks, transportation networks, communications, health and medical care, schools, and the other basic infrastructure.

PHOTOJOURNALISM A form of journalism that uses primarily photographs rather than the printed word to tell a story, describe an event, or establish a mood.

Biographies and Organizations
World Leadership and Unclear Mission

DIEM, NGO DINH

When the Geneva Accords gave South and North Vietnam independence from France in 1954, Ngo Dinh Diem, a fiercely anti-Communist Catholic in a traditionally Buddhist nation, became prime minister of South Vietnam. The following year, he ousted Emperor Bao Dai in a rigged referendum and assumed sole leadership of the country. His rule was to be one marked with contradictions. A devoutly religious man, Diem governed over an increasingly corrupt and repressive regime until 1963, when his generals overthrew and assassinated him.

EISENHOWER, DWIGHT D.

President Dwight D. Eisenhower works in the Oval Office on April 1, 1960.

For almost twenty years, Dwight David Eisenhower, as supreme commander of the Allied forces in Europe during World War II, commander of North Atlantic Treaty Organization (NATO) forces from 1950 to 1952, and president of the United States from 1953 to 1961, played a major role in the events that shaped the 20th century.

Dwight D. Eisenhower Library

Eisenhower was born on October 14, 1890 in Denison, Texas, but grew up in Abilene, Kansas. He graduated from West Point in 1915 and in 1933 became Army Chief of Staff General Douglas MacArthur's administrative assistant. Lieutenant Colonel Eisenhower attracted considerable public attention in 1941 when the troops he commanded in huge war-game maneuvers in Louisiana defeated their opponents through the careful coordination of infantry, tank, and airplane forces.

Biographies and Organizations
World Leadership and Unclear Mission, cont.

Promoted to brigadier general, Eisenhower returned to Washington after the attack by the Japanese on Pearl Harbor to be the assistant chief of staff to George C. Marshall. In this position, he helped draft the U.S. military's World War II global strategy, outlined a plan for a cross-English Channel invasion of France, and designed the European theater of operations command that he was appointed to lead in June, 1942. As supreme commander of the Allied Expeditionary Forces in World War II, Eisenhower directed the invasions of North Africa, Italy, France, and Germany.

After Germany's defeat, Eisenhower oversaw the demobilization of American troops before leaving the service to become president of Columbia University in 1948. In 1950, President Harry Truman appointed Eisenhower supreme commander of NATO, a position he held until his decision to seek the Republican nomination for president in 1952. Eisenhower defeated Democratic challenger Adlai Stevenson by a large plurality of more than six million votes.

Eisenhower's administration is remembered chiefly for its lack of legislative initiatives and calm style of consensus management during a period of national prosperity. In foreign policy, the Eisenhower years stand out as a period of relative peace. One month after his election in 1952, Eisenhower traveled to Korea and halted the fighting through an uneasy truce with North Korea. For much of his eight-year administration, he avoided stark confrontations with the Soviet Union; he even hoped to improve U.S.–Soviet relations to the point where the two superpowers might contemplate weapons reductions. Nevertheless, Eisenhower could not escape the realities of the Cold War. He involved the United States in the affairs of Asian, Middle Eastern, and Latin

American nations in the pursuit of U.S. Cold War objectives. In 1954, Eisenhower committed the United States to the Southeast Asia Treaty Organization (SEATO) to protect Southeast Asian nations from Communist attack. This commitment helped to draw the United States ever deeper into the war between the Communists and non-Communists in Vietnam.

Eisenhower suffered a heart attack in September, 1955 but returned to his duties within two months' time. He ran for reelection in 1956, once again against Stevenson, and won in a landslide. Popular and beloved by Americans after leaving the White House, Eisenhower retired to his farm in Gettysburg, Pennsylvania, in 1961. He suffered another serious heart attack in 1965 and died four years later on March 28, 1969.

JOHNSON, LYNDON B.

Yoichi R. Okamoto/ LBJ Library Collection

Lyndon B. Johnson, one of the most controversial U.S. presidents of modern times, fought for African American equality more than any president since Abraham Lincoln and sought to use the nation's wealth to eradicate poverty. Johnson also increased the U.S. commitment to one of the worst foreign policy disasters in the nation's history, the Vietnam War.

Raised in Johnson City, Texas, Johnson was born on August 27, 1908 into a financially poor family with a rich political heritage. Johnson graduated from Southwest Texas State Teachers College in 1930 and briefly taught school before embarking on his political career. In 1937, while campaigning as a fervent supporter of fellow Democrat Franklin D. Roosevelt, Johnson was elected to the U.S. House of Representatives.

Biographies and Organizations
World Leadership and Unclear Mission, cont.

In 1948, Johnson was elected to the Senate and in 1953, he became minority leader. In 1954, when he was reelected along with enough other Democrats for his party to regain control of the Senate, Johnson became majority leader. After recovering from a heart attack in 1955, he continued his policy of working with President Dwight D. Eisenhower in formulating bipartisan policies. Johnson's ability to search for the common ground upon which a compromise could be reached enabled him to become one of the most powerful men in Washington.

In 1960, Democratic presidential candidate John F. Kennedy offered the vice presidential position to Johnson. It was assumed the proud Johnson would decline the offer, but instead he accepted. Although Johnson participated in Cabinet meetings and chaired several important committees as vice president, he was clearly unhappy in the office. He felt restricted by the limited powers of the vice president, and he hated the personal style of the president and his brother Robert F. Kennedy. They, in turn, despised him. Then, on November 22, 1963, Kennedy was assassinated in Dallas, Texas, and Johnson assumed the office of president.

Adroitly capitalizing on the somber mood of the nation, Johnson swiftly achieved enactment of civil rights legislation and a tax cut program— legislation Kennedy had sought before his death—as a living memorial to the murdered president. His success with the Congress and promise that the United States would not become involved in Vietnam, enabled him to easily win reelection in 1964. The election also secured a large Democratic majority in both houses of Congress.

Claiming that the election was a mandate to create his vision of a "Great Society," Johnson began working to secure passage of a number of important programs and bills in 1965. These included Medicare, a system of health insurance for the elderly under the Social Security program, and the Voting Rights Act of 1965, which outlawed illiteracy tests that had been used to prevent African Americans from voting. As part of Johnson's War on Poverty program, Congress increased unemployment benefits, expanded the food-stamp program, created new youth employment opportunities, and provided legal services to the poor (Legal Services) and special preschool classes to underprivileged children (Head Start). These programs amounted to the most ambitious attempt at liberal reform since the New Deal.

Johnson's success in domestic affairs was not matched in the foreign policy arena. By 1966, he had committed almost half a million U.S. troops to the defense of South Vietnam, and U.S. planes were bombing North Vietnam. As victory in Vietnam seemed to slip further away and casualties mounted, Johnson's popularity weakened along with his political power. After the surprising primary election success of Democratic Senator Eugene McCarthy in 1968 and the entry into the race of Senator Robert Kennedy, a demoralized Johnson stunned the nation with his televised announcement that he would not seek another term as president. Johnson died four years after leaving office, on January 22, 1973.

Biographies and Organizations
World Leadership and Unclear Mission, cont.

*Library of Congress,
Prints & Photographs Division*

KENNEDY, JOHN F.

President John F. Kennedy, 1961.

The administration of John Fitzgerald Kennedy, famous for its youth and style, ushered in a period of hope, vigor, and commitment for the United States that would be cruelly cut short by his assassination.

Kennedy, the youngest man ever elected president of the United States, was born in Brookline, Massachusetts on May 29, 1917 into a large Irish Catholic family. He graduated from Harvard College in 1940 and enlisted in the U.S. Navy the next year. In 1943, after the PT boat he was commanding was sunk by a Japanese destroyer, he heroically saved the life of one of his crew members. In the process, however, he aggravated a chronic back ailment that plagued him for the rest of his life.

In 1946, Kennedy was elected as a Massachusetts Democrat to his first of three terms in the U.S. House of Representatives. In 1952, he defeated incumbent Henry Cabot Lodge Jr., for a seat in the U.S. Senate. The next year, he married Washington socialite Jacqueline Bouvier and, while recuperating from back surgery, wrote *Profiles in Courage*, a book of political sketches that won the Pulitzer Prize.

After an unsuccessful attempt to become Adlai Stevenson's vice presidential running mate in 1956, Kennedy's political career was buoyed by an exceptionally wide victory margin in his reelection to the Senate in 1958. He won the Democratic Party presidential nomination in 1960 and ran against the Republican vice president Richard Nixon. Kennedy was narrowly elected by a margin of only 118,550 popular votes out of 68.3 million votes cast.

As president, he projected an image of a leader directly involved in formulating national and international policy. Domestic politics were dominated by the economy and the Civil Rights Movement. Kennedy endorsed the use of tax cuts and increases in government spending to stimulate the economy. Kennedy's greatest success as president was his handling of the 1962 Cuban Missile Crisis. He also rose to the challenge of Soviet pressure over Berlin, but Vietnam was a nemesis with which he struggled until his tragic assassination in Dallas, Texas, on November 22, 1963.

MINH, HO CHI

Despite his seemingly frail appearance, Ho Chi Minh possessed an iron will and was singularly determined to liberate his country from foreign colonial powers. He never lived to see the final victory, but his three decades of uncompromising leadership placed Vietnam on the path to national unity under a Communist government.

Ho was born Nguyen Sinh Cung on May 19, 1890. Indochina was then under French colonial supervision and suffering from the effects of this outside domination. Ho came to resent colonialism and dedicated his life to ending it in Vietnam.

After helping to create an effective guerrilla movement, the Viet Minh, to fight the Japanese in World War II, Ho stepped into a power vacuum that was left by the absence of any imperial power in Vietnam at the end of the conflict. On September 2, 1945, Ho declared the creation of the Democratic Republic of Vietnam with himself as president. After eight years of fighting, the Viet Minh decisively defeated the French at the Battle of Dien Bien Phu, and the French withdrew from Indochina.

Biographies and Organizations
World Leadership and Unclear Mission, cont.

Subsequent negotiations at Geneva, Switzerland, in 1954 acknowledged Ho's complete control of the northern half of Vietnam but also recognized the regime of the non-Communist government in the southern half. Reunification of the country was to take place via a national election. Ho was easily the most popular man throughout the country and would have easily won the contest, which is why the Ngo Dinh Diem regime in South Vietnam, backed by the U.S. government, never allowed it to occur.

Ho continued consolidating his power in the North until 1960, when he initiated a concerted guerrilla strategy to give support to the Communists in South Vietnam and topple its increasingly unpopular government. In many respects, it was less a war than a terrorist campaign directed against political adversaries. Ho succeeded in convincing his countrymen that the very presence of U.S. forces constituted a new imperialist force that must be defeated. Ho was also skilled at the delicate balancing of politics with the Soviet Union and China, bitter ideological rivals that both provided material and military assistance. Ho did not survive to see the fruits of his labors; he died of a heart ailment on September 2, 1969.

NIXON, RICHARD M.

Library of Congress

After finally achieving his dream of becoming president in 1968, Richard Milhous Nixon became the first U.S. chief executive to resign from office. It was a dramatic ending to a long and controversial political career marked by early unscrupulous election campaign tactics and later foreign policy accomplishments.

Nixon was born on January 9, 1913 in Yorba Linda, California. He graduated from the small Quaker-run Whittier College in 1934 and completed his law studies at Duke University in 1937. After serving in the U.S. Navy during World War II, Nixon entered California politics and was elected to the U.S. House of Representatives in 1946. In Congress, Nixon won a national reputation for his aggressive behavior as a member of the House Un-American Activities Committee (HUAC). Capitalizing on his notoriety, Nixon successfully ran for a seat in the U.S. Senate in 1950.

Nixon's youth, anti-communist reputation, and California residence made him an ideal running mate for Dwight D. Eisenhower in 1952. Nixon assumed the task of pacifying various Republican Party groups and took many overseas goodwill trips during his eight years as vice president. In 1960, Nixon easily won the Republican nomination for president, but he was defeated in the general election by Democrat John F. Kennedy in a very close race. Two years later, Nixon ran for governor of California and lost badly to the Democratic incumbent. However, Nixon made a remarkable political comeback in 1968. This time, running for president against Democrat Hubert H. Humphrey and third-party candidate George Wallace, he won.

Nixon assumed the presidency in 1969 at a difficult time in U.S. history. High inflation, domestic civil rights protests, and the Vietnam War had split the nation along age, class, and racial lines. During his first term, Nixon gradually withdrew U.S. forces from South Vietnam. Under this "Vietnamization" plan, the South Vietnamese army was trained to take over the fighting and to use American air power to force North Vietnam to relinquish its quest for total victory. In 1970,

Biographies and Organizations
World Leadership and Unclear Mission, cont.

American bombing of Communist bases in Cambodia and Laos succeeded in disrupting enemy supply lines but unleashed a fury of domestic political protest. In January 1973, after massive American B-52 bombing attacks, North Vietnam agreed to a negotiated peace. This "peace with honor" turned out to be little more than an opportunity for the United States to pull out of a war it could not win, however. South Vietnam fell under the domination of the North in 1975. In addition, the bombing had dramatically enlarged the area of conflict in Indochina, undermining sources of stability in Cambodia and giving an opening for the Khmer Rouge and their policies of mass murder.

Nixon's other foreign policy achievements were less controversial. Pursuing a policy of peaceful coexistence called *détente,* he improved relations with the Soviet Union. Nixon also visited the People's Republic of China in 1972, thereby opening communications with that country and substantially reducing tensions in the world. During the 1973 Yom Kippur War, the Nixon administration, along with the Soviet Union, successfully pressured Israel, Egypt, and Syria to cease hostilities.

In domestic politics, Nixon's efforts to curtail the federal government's role in civil rights advocacy and social welfare provision met with mixed results. He dismantled many liberal programs of the 1960s and slowed down the progress of school integration. Yet the Democratic Congress blocked his legislation to prohibit forced busing and stymied numerous attempts to cut social programs. Nixon, moreover, sometimes initiated policies more liberal than conservative, as in his imposition of wage and price controls in 1971 and his Family Assistance Plan proposal of 1970.

Partially out of a desire to stop leaks of classified Vietnam War-related information to the press and out of a desire to ensure his own reelection in 1972, Nixon authorized the establishment of a team of agents to tap telephones illegally and burglarize the offices of opponents. When they were caught in the Democratic Party's national campaign office in the Watergate building in Washington, D.C. in June, 1972 and arrested, Nixon authorized the payment of large sums of campaign contribution money to maintain their silence and promised them clemency after the election. In the fall, Nixon was re-elected by an overwhelming majority against his Democratic rival, George McGovern.

Shortly after Nixon began his second term, the cover-up Nixon had authorized of the activities of the clandestine break-in began to unravel. During the next two years, Nixon and the nation experienced his gradual political destruction. A nationally televised Senate investigation piled up evidence of his guilt in obstructing justice and in abusing the powers and privileges of his office for personal and political gain. Faced with certain impeachment by Congress for his involvement in the Watergate cover-up, Nixon resigned on August 8, 1974.

One month later, President Gerald Ford granted Nixon a full pardon from any federal prosecution. Nixon accepted the pardon but never admitted that he had ever done anything illegal. He died in New York City on April 22, 1994.

Biographies and Organizations
World Leadership and Unclear Mission, cont.

SOUTHEAST ASIA TREATY ORGANIZATION (SEATO)

The Southeast Asia Treaty Organization (SEATO) was created in 1954 to ensure the security of the nations of Southeast Asia and Oceania that were allied with the Western powers. It was disbanded in 1977.

SEATO members were Australia, Britain, France, New Zealand, Pakistan, the Philippines, Thailand, and the United States. The organization implemented the provisions of two treaties: the Manila Pact, or Southeast Asia Collective Defense Treaty, which established a military alliance against Communist threats to the sovereignty of the member nations; and the Pacific Charter, in which signatories pledged to uphold the principle of self-determination and to promote better living standards and social well-being. Despite the economic and social provisions of the Pacific Charter, SEATO remained primarily a collective defense organization.

SEATO decisions were required to carry unanimously, but this made it easy for dissent to hinder its effectiveness. The organization failed to deal collectively with problems in Vietnam, Laos, and other nations, and its reputation was harmed by suggestions of its neocolonialist purposes—that the Western powers were using it to control the less powerful member states. SEATO was disbanded by mutual consent of its members in June, 1977.

VIET CONG (VC)

The National Front for the Liberation of South Vietnam, usually known as the National Liberation Front (NLF) or Viet Cong (VC), was formed on December 20, 1960. It was a political/guerrilla group backed by North Vietnam that operated in South Vietnam to topple the U.S.-backed South Vietnamese government. During the Vietnam War, it also tried to force the American military out of South Vietnam.

From the birth of the Viet Cong in 1960, Washington policy makers claimed that North Vietnam alone directed the armed struggle in South Vietnam. Key members of the administrations of President John F. Kennedy and President Lyndon B. Johnson argued that the flow of troops and supplies from North to South kept the revolution alive. This remained the underpinning of the official explanation for U.S. involvement in the Vietnam War and provided its justification. Those who opposed U.S. intervention argued that the insurgency was essentially a civil war. They suggested that the Viet Cong was a Southern organization that had risen at Southern initiative in response to Southern demands.

The Viet Cong was a classic Communist-front organization comprising Communists and non-Communists. It was organized with the purpose of mobilizing the anti-President Diem forces in Southern society. The Viet Cong made temporary alliances with all elements of Southern society that opposed American intervention and the Saigon regime.

The Viet Cong reached its zenith during the 1968 Tet Offensive when it launched a coordinated attack against key urban centers throughout the South. Although it suffered tremendous military losses, the Viet Cong gained a tremendous psychological victory over the Americans and their Saigon allies. Shortly after the Tet Offensive, peace talks opened in Paris.

In 1969, the Viet Cong oversaw the creation of a government-in-waiting, the Provisional Revolutionary Government (PRG). The PRG hoped to come to full power in the South after the political and military struggles were concluded. But as the war dragged on, the People's Army of Vietnam (PAVN; North Vietnam) conventional forces played a more active role in the Southern strategy. After the fall of Saigon, only a handful of Viet Cong officials were incorporated into the new national government.

Places and Things
World Leadership and Unclear Mission

CONTAINMENT DOCTRINE (1947)

In July, 1947, U.S. ambassador to the Soviet Union George F. Kennan published an article in the journal *Foreign Affairs* and signed it simply "X." The essay articulated his policy of containing Communism where it already existed at that time and actively preventing its spread to other countries. Although the article was published anonymously, Kennan's authorship was quickly established. Dubbed the "Containment Doctrine," this policy became the foundation of U.S. policy during the Cold War and was behind U.S. efforts in Vietnam.

HO CHI MINH TRAIL

The Ho Chi Minh Trail was a network of roads that stretched from North Vietnam through eastern Laos to South Vietnam, forming the main supply route for troops and material that supported the North's war effort. The North Vietnamese forces were able to keep this vital supply route open throughout the Vietnam War.

PARIS PEACE ACCORD (1973)

Signed on January 27, 1973, the Paris Peace Accord officially ended U.S. involvement in the Vietnam War and established a schedule for the withdrawal of U.S. troops and the exchange of prisoners. Although the agreement initiated a cease-fire that began the next day, the United States did not withdraw all of its troops until April 30, 1975, when the South Vietnamese surrendered to North Vietnam and the city of Saigon fell to the Communists.

RICHARD NIXON'S "SILENT MAJORITY" SPEECH (1969)

On November 3, 1969, U.S. President Richard Nixon addressed the American people in a televised speech regarding the Vietnam War. In the address, Nixon presented his plan for ending the conflict, including the implementation of his "Vietnamization" plan, and called on "the great silent majority" of Americans to support his efforts.

SOUTHEAST ASIA

An ethnically and culturally diverse area of the largest continent,
Southeast Asia lies south of China and between the Pacific and Indian
Oceans. Southeast Asia encompasses the nations of Vietnam, Thailand,
Laos, Cambodia, Myanmar, Malaysia, and the island nations of
Singapore, Indonesia, Brunei, and the Philippines.

TONKIN GULF RESOLUTION (1964)

The Tonkin Gulf Resolution of 1964 was the closest Congress came to
endorsing American participation in the Vietnam War. Unlike previous
resolutions, the Tonkin Gulf Resolution, which Congress passed on
August 7, 1964, did not require Congress to authorize presidential
action, but only to "approve and support" any actions that the
president found necessary. That change in wording indicated a new
shift in Congress' role during wartime. No longer the ultimate
authority, Congress was to provide only subordinate support to the
chief executive. Congress repealed the resolution on January 2, 1971
and concern about the Vietnam conflict and congressional war powers
in general eventually led to the passage of the War Powers Resolution
of 1973.

VIET CONG PROGRAM (1962)

The Viet Cong were Communist rebels supported by North Vietnam
who worked in South Vietnam during the Vietnam War. In January,
1962, the organization issued the following declaration to the
Vietnamese people, outlining its program for revolution and reform in
South Vietnam.

1. We will overthrow the Ngo Dinh Diem government and form a
   national democratic coalition government.

2. We will carry out a program involving extension of democratic
   liberties, general amnesty for political detainees, abolition of
   agrovilles and resettlement centers, abolition of the special military
   tribunal law, and other undemocratic laws.

Places and Things
World Leadership and Unclear Mission, cont.

3. We will abolish the economic monopoly of the United States and its henchmen, protect domestically made products, promote development of the economy, and allow forced evacuees from North Vietnam to return to their place of birth.

4. We will reduce land rent and prepare for land reform.

5. We will eliminate U.S. cultural enslavement and depravity and build a nationalistic progressive culture and education.

6. We will abolish the system of American military advisers and close all foreign military bases in Vietnam.

7. We will establish equality between men and women and among different nationalities and recognize the autonomous rights of the national minorities in the country.

8. We will pursue a foreign policy of peace and will establish diplomatic relations with all countries that respect the independence and sovereignty of Vietnam.

9. We will reestablish normal relations between North and South as a first step toward peaceful reunification of the country.

10. We will oppose aggressive wars and actively defend world peace.

"VIETNAMIZATION"
In 1969, U.S. President Richard Nixon began replacing American troops with South Vietnamese troops—a process known as "Vietnamization"—as a way to transfer military responsibility to South Vietnam and begin the withdrawal of American forces.

Events and Eras
World Leadership and Unclear Mission

COLD WAR (1945–1989)

"Let us not be deceived—today we are in the midst of a cold war."
Thus spoke Bernard Baruch, a wealthy financier and presidential adviser,
in a speech in April, 1947. He had coined the term that would come to
define the monumental struggle between the United States and its allies
and the Soviet Union and its partners that began shortly after the end
of World War II and continued until the dissolution of the Soviet Union
in 1989. Based on fundamental ideological differences, a deep-seated
distrust of each other, and an escalating arms race, the Cold War shaped
the international world order for more than forty years and profoundly
influenced the politics and economies of many nations.

The arms race fueled by the Cold War was expensive and dangerous—
costing both the United States and the Soviet Union billions of dollars,
and bringing questionable security at best. Many peace advocates
thought that the arms buildup was a greater threat to the United
States than the Soviets were and advocated bilateral or even unilateral
arms reductions in an effort to diminish the ever-growing threat of
nuclear war.

This threat became frighteningly real in 1962, when the Soviets
attempted to put missiles in Cuba. Following a short standoff, during
which President John F. Kennedy threatened nuclear retaliation, the
Soviets agreed to withdraw their missiles in return for Kennedy's
promise not to invade Cuba. Both nations were sufficiently frightened
by this episode that they began a period of de-escalation, commonly
called *détente*. This period lasted from 1963 to 1980, when the Soviets

Events and Eras
World Leadership and Unclear Mission, cont.

invaded Afghanistan and the United States elected Ronald Reagan president. These events reignited the arms race and the Cold War until 1985, when Mikhail Gorbachev came to power in the Soviet Union. Gorbachev sought to ease tensions with the West while relaxing internal controls within the Soviet system. Within four years, Gorbachev's policies of *glasnost* and *perestroika* led to the downfall of Communism, first in the Soviet satellite nations, and then in the Soviet Union itself, which was dissolved into many independent states. Although most observers consider the dissolution of the U.S.S.R. to mark the end of the Cold War, both the United States and Russia (as well as several other former Soviet states) maintain significant nuclear arsenals. Thus, although the tensions of the Cold War are significantly reduced, the threat of nuclear war is not absent.

INDOCHINA WAR (1946–1954)
Also known as the "French War," the Indochina War was fought by Vietnamese nationalists under Ho Chi Minh to prevent France from continuing to control its Vietnamese and Cambodian colony, Cochinchina. Victory in the conflict provided independence for North Vietnam, but international agreements at the Geneva Conference of 1954 divided Vietnam into northern and southern zones. The United States supported South Vietnam during the subsequent Vietnam War, whereas North Vietnam embraced Communism and sought assistance from China and the Soviet Union to reunify Vietnam.

The Indochina War began in the port city of Haiphong on
November 20, 1946, when Vietnamese troops (known as the Viet
Minh) attacked French civilians in the hope of drawing the French
colonial army, weakened by war with Japan and Germany, into open
battle. One month later, Viet Minh militia and regular army units
suffered heavy losses after staging military assaults on French installa-
tions in Tonkin, Hue, and Hanoi. More powerful than the ill-equipped
Vietnamese troops, the French forces maintained control of major cities,
which forced Ho and his army to seek safe haven in the elevated
mountain and jungle region of Viet Bac. In the south, the French experienced less difficulty in initially stifling Vietnamese resistance, though
urban terrorism hampered their control of Saigon.

Although possessing more troops and sophisticated military equipment
than the Viet Minh, French forces suffered from a high rate of turnover
in leadership and unclear policy goals. In contrast, the Vietnamese
united behind the spirited leadership of the nationalist hero Ho. By the
early 1950s, the Viet Minh grew to more than 350,000. Bolstered by a
larger force, Vietnamese military leaders began to use conventional
military tactics to attempt to oust the French from bases in Tonkin, the
Mekong Delta, and the Central Highlands. Those efforts culminated in
the Battle of Dien Bien Phu on May 7, 1954. One of the most effective
and devastating conventional military sieges in 20th-century history,
Dien Bien Phu resulted in 3,000 dead and 10,000 prisoners (half of
whom were wounded). Encircled by heavy artillery transported by
Vietnamese bicycles, the entire French garrison surrendered.

Events and Eras
World Leadership and Unclear Mission, cont.

France and the Viet Minh met at the Geneva Conference of 1954 to settle the eight-year conflict. The so-called Geneva Accords divided Vietnam at the 17th parallel and ended forever a French presence in what had been known as Indochina. By April, 1956, all French forces had left Vietnam.

TONKIN GULF INCIDENTS (1964)

The Tonkin Gulf incidents were major events that prompted the Tonkin Gulf Resolution and helped bring about the Vietnam War.

On July 31, 1964, the destroyer USS *Maddox* started a reconnaissance cruise off the coast of North Vietnam. About the time of the cruise, the United States also scheduled a string of covert operations against the North Vietnamese coast carried out by relatively small vessels as part of a program called Operation Plan 34A (OPLAN 34A). One of the *Maddox*'s main missions was to learn about North Vietnamese coastal defenses, and it was apparently believed that more would be learned if those defenses were in an aroused state during the patrol.

On the afternoon of August 2, three North Vietnamese torpedo boats came out from the island and attacked the *Maddox*. The attack was unsuccessful, and the torpedo boats suffered varying degrees of damage and crew casualties. President Lyndon B. Johnson decided not to order any further retaliation, partly because he had reason to believe that the attack had been a result of confusion in the North Vietnamese chain of command rather than a deliberate decision by the government in Hanoi.

On August 3, the *Maddox* and another destroyer, the USS *C. Turner Joy*, went back into the Gulf of Tonkin to resume the patrol; they were operating under orders more cautious than those with which *Maddox* had gone into the gulf on July 31. Many sailors on the destroyers thought that another attack by North Vietnamese torpedo boats was likely. For about two hours on the night of August 4, such an attack seemed to be in progress, but the situation was very confused. Those who were aboard the destroyers that night are still divided on the issue; some think that they were attacked by torpedo boats, but others think that what appeared on their radar screens was nothing but weather-generated anomalies, seagulls, foam on the crests of waves, or other natural disturbances. The overall weight of the evidence is with those who deny that an attack occurred.

In Washington, after some initial uncertainty, it was decided that there had been a genuine attack. Intercepted North Vietnamese radio messages seemed to provide the clinching evidence. The texts of the messages have never been released; it seems likely that they were actually descriptions of the combat between *Maddox* and the three torpedo boats on August 2, and were misinterpreted by the Americans as references to a more recent event.

President Johnson, believing that an attack had occurred, ordered retaliatory air strikes. He also asked for and quickly obtained a congressional resolution (the Tonkin Gulf Resolution), passed almost unanimously, which authorized him to do whatever was necessary to deal with Communist aggression in Vietnam. The Tonkin Gulf incidents were politically very profitable for Johnson in the short run because of the

Events and Eras
World Leadership and Unclear Mission, cont.

overwhelming public approval of the way he had handled the crisis. In the long run, however, the cost to the president's credibility was considerable. It became clear that Congress and the public had been misled about the administration's intentions and about the relationship between the OPLAN 34A raids and the Tonkin Gulf incidents.

MY LAI MASSACRE

The My Lai Massacre on March 16, 1968 was the most notorious U.S. military atrocity of the Vietnam War. Equally infamous was the cover-up of the incident perpetrated by the brigade and division staffs.

Located in the Quang Ngai Province, My Lai was one of a cluster of South Vietnamese hamlets making up Son My village. To snare the estimated 250 Viet Cong (VC) operating in the area, U.S. soldiers were ordered to conduct a classic search-and-destroy sweep, which had to date been characterized by lightly scattered direct VC contact and a high rate of friendly losses to snipers, mines, and booby-trap incidents.

The airmobile assault into My Lai was timed to arrive shortly after the local women had departed for market. The soldiers had expected to engage elements of one of the most successful VC units in the area but instead found only women, children, and old men. The U.S. soldiers ran wild, particularly those commanded by First Lieutenant William Calley. They indiscriminately shot people as they ran from their huts and then systematically rounded up survivors, allegedly leading them to a nearby ditch and executing them. More villagers were killed as huts and bunkers were destroyed by fire and explosives. The killing was reportedly halted only when Hugh Thompson, an aeroscout pilot supporting the operation, landed his helicopter between the Americans and fleeing Vietnamese and confronted the U.S. soldiers. Between 200 and 500 Vietnamese civilians were massacred in the incident. Because of false reporting and the subsequent cover-up, actual casualty figures are difficult to substantiate.

The incident, uncovered a year later, was investigated by the Army Criminal Investigation Division and an army board of inquiry, headed by Lieutenant General William Peers. Although the findings of the board did not ascribe causes for the massacre, many have cited the frustrations of soldiers too long faced with unanswerable losses of comrades, poor leadership from the division commander on down the ranks, and the measurement of success by the statistical yardstick of enemy body count.

Although the Peers report produced a list of thirty persons who knew of the atrocities, only fourteen were charged with crimes. All eventually had their charges dismissed or were acquitted by courts-martial except for Calley, who was found guilty of murdering twenty-two civilians and sentenced to life imprisonment. Proclaimed by much of the public as a scapegoat, Calley's sentence was twice reduced—eventually to ten years—and after serving about one-third of his sentence, he was paroled by U.S. President Richard Nixon in November, 1974.

TET OFFENSIVE

The Tet Offensive of 1968 was a decisive and psychological turning point of the Vietnam War. Although U.S. and South Vietnamese forces emerged victorious from the countrywide Communist attacks, the costly victory convinced many in the United States that increased American intervention would not break the will of the Communists.

Events and Eras
World Leadership and Unclear Mission, cont.

Militarily, the Vietnam War had not been going well for the Communist Viet Cong (VC) and the North Vietnamese People's Army of Vietnam (PAVN), who were unable to compete with U.S. military firepower and mobility. As a result, Democratic Republic of Vietnam (DRV, North Vietnam) defense minister General Vo Nguyen Giap sought to end the war in one master stroke. Giap's plan, borrowed from Chinese Communist doctrine, was based on the concept of the "General Offensive." The General Offensive was set for Tet 1968, the beginning of the lunar new year, the most important holiday for the Vietnamese.

Giap's buildup and staging for the Tet Offensive was a masterpiece of deception. Starting in the fall of 1967, Giap implemented a "peripheral campaign" to draw U.S. combat units out of the urban areas and toward the borders. From January 21, 1968 until the point when countrywide attacks erupted at Tet, the attention of most of the U.S. military was riveted on PAVN attacks on Khe Sanh, an isolated U.S. Marine outpost. Meanwhile, the Communists used the Christmas 1967 cease-fire to move their forces into position, while senior commanders gathered reconnaissance on their assigned objectives. Lieutenant General Frederick Weyand was not thrown off by the peripheral campaign. On January 10, 1968, Weyand pulled more U.S. combat battalions back in around Saigon. As a result, there were twenty-seven battalions (instead of the planned fourteen) in the Saigon area when the attack came.

The countrywide Communist attacks were set to commence on January 31, 1968, but Giap's secret buildup cost him in terms of coordination. The attack happened twenty-four hours prematurely, as VC commanders followed the lunar calendar in effect in South Vietnam rather than a new lunar calendar proclaimed by the North Vietnamese leadership for all of Vietnam. That resulted in the cancellation of the Tet holiday cease-fire; South Vietnamese troops were called back to their units, and U.S. forces went on alert. Giap had lost the element of surprise.

In the early morning of January 31, the Presidential Palace in Saigon was attacked, and soon, the city of Hue was under attack. Before the day was over, five of six autonomous cities, thirty-six of forty-four provincial capitals, and sixty-four of two-hundred-forty-five district capitals were under attack. With the exception of Khe Sanh, the ancient capital of Hue, and the area around Saigon, the fighting was over in a few days. Militarily, the Tet Offensive was a disaster for the Communists. Giap was unable to exploit his element of surprise; by attacking every- where, he had superior strength nowhere. The Tet Offensive was also a tremendous loss for the VC. Although a large portion of the PAVN conducted the feint at Khe Sanh, VC guerrilla forces had led the major attacks in the south, and they suffered the heaviest casualties. The guerrilla infrastructure developed over so many years was wiped out. After Tet 1968, the war was run entirely by North Vietnam, and the VC were never again a significant force on the battlefield. When Saigon fell in 1975, it was to four North Vietnamese army corps.

The United States had delivered the Communists a crushing tactical defeat, but the U.S. public—doubtful that the Communists were as weak as the U.S. military had been claiming, as well as shocked by the brutality shown on television during the offensive—had begun to believe that the war was unwinnable. Thus, the Tet Offensive is one of the most paradoxical of history's decisive battles.

HO CHI MINH CAMPAIGN (1975)

The Ho Chi Minh Campaign, an April, 1975 attack on Saigon, gave the Democratic Republic of Vietnam (DRV, North Vietnam) the decisive victory it had fought so long to achieve. The Communists' triumph spelled the end of the Vietnam War.

Encouraged by the partial collapse of the Army of the Republic of Vietnam (ARVN, South Vietnam) in early 1975, the Communist Hanoi Politburo decided that the South Vietnamese capital of Saigon should

Events and Eras
World Leadership and Unclear Mission, cont.

be taken before the 1975 rainy season rather than the following year. The plan was to achieve victory in the Ho Chi Minh Campaign before the late Ho Chi Minh's birthday on May 19.

Xuan Loc fell on April 21; by April 25, South Vietnamese ARVN forces around Saigon were under pressure from all sides. The People's Army of Vietnam (PAVN, North Vietnam) attack on Saigon began on April 26 with artillery bombardments and a ground assault. PAVN forces also occupied Nhon Trach, southeast of Saigon, which enabled them to bring 130-millimeter artillery to bear on Tan Son Nhut airport. On April 27, they cut Route 4, but South Vietnamese ARVN forces fought back by counterattacking sappers who had seized bridges and by putting up stiff resistance.

By April 28, Communist forces had pushed forward their attack by positioning units for the final assault and successfully attacking ARVN units in bases surrounding Saigon. A full evacuation was initially delayed for fear of its negative impact on morale. When the evacuation did begin on April 29, the final U.S. pullout was chaotic—a poorly organized swirl of vehicles and crowds trying to connect with helicopters, ships, and planes. In the confusion, the Americans left many Vietnamese employees behind, and as few as a third of the individuals and families deemed to be at risk were evacuated or managed to escape.

Units around Saigon came under heavy attack on April 29. While some Communist PAVN units held outlying South Vietnamese garrisons in check, other North Vietnamese forces moved toward the center of the city and key targets. Although some South Vietnamese ARVN units continued to resist, they could not slow the North Vietnamese PAVN advance; on April 30, ARVN forces were ordered to cease fighting. Against such a strong opponent, the Saigon government proved incapable of continued resistance without active U.S. support. The Ho Chi Minh Campaign had achieved its goal.

Background
World Leadership and Unclear Mission

VIETNAM WAR

Marking one of the most traumatic periods of U.S. history, the Vietnam War spanned more than a decade and caused massive disruption both in Southeast Asia and on the American home front. Although U.S. leaders were often ambiguous about American involvement in Vietnam, they nevertheless pursued a fairly unbroken policy of interference in the country in an effort to halt the spread of communism during the Cold War. In the end, the U.S. defeat in Vietnam proved costly, both financially and in the number of lives lost, and diminished America's reputation as the defender of democracy and freedom throughout the world.

When the French moved into Indochina in the mid-nineteenth century to capitalize on trade potential in Asia, the U.S. government voiced concern that the French posed a threat to American interests in China. Nevertheless, the French quickly colonized Indochina (primarily the country of Vietnam), holding control over this Asian colony for nearly a century, despite a growing nationalist movement within Vietnam led by a group known as the Viet Minh, under the leadership of Ho Chi Minh.

Although America continued to show its disapproval of France's colonial domination of Indochina through World War II, by 1945, growing fear of Soviet activity worldwide prompted the United States to reverse its position and support French colonialism in Southeast Asia. When the nationalist movement, led by the devoted nationalist figure Ho Chi Minh, threatened to topple the French government right after World War II and usher in a Communist regime, President Harry Truman committed limited U.S. resources to assist the French in reestablishing their presence in Vietnam.

Background
World Leadership and Unclear Mission, cont.

On September 2, 1945, Ho proclaimed Vietnam's independence from the French. Although the French government and Ho held a series of talks in an attempt to negotiate a settlement, such efforts proved fruitless, and fighting erupted between the two sides in December, 1946. The French military effort went badly and opposition to the war grew among the population in France. For that reason, the French government began to talk about hammering out a negotiated settlement with the Vietnamese, a resolve that was further strengthened by French military reverses in May, 1954, most notably at the Battle of Dien Bien Phu. At peace talks held in Geneva, Switzerland, the French agreed to a gradual withdrawal and the country was divided into North and South regions until open elections could be held to allow the Vietnamese to select their new political leaders. The Geneva Accords marked the beginning of the end of French influence in the region, which was almost entirely withdrawn by 1956.

With the French capitulation at Geneva in 1954, the United States, by its own decision, assumed responsibility for South Vietnam. Long frustrated with the French, both for their political handling of Indochina and for what was perceived as their weak military performance against Ho Chi Minh's Viet Minh, the United States sought to play the decisive hand in the future of the area. At first, President Dwight D. Eisenhower attempted to work with the French and other Western allies to contain Communism, which had already firmly established itself in North Vietnam, in Southeast Asia. He and Secretary of State John Foster Dulles engineered the Southeast Asia Treaty Organization (SEATO) in September, 1954, which under a separate protocol gave Laos, Cambodia, and South Vietnam a special protected status.

In the spring of 1955, Eisenhower abandoned the allied approach and moved in a unilateral direction as the United States dedicated itself to building a strong Vietnamese nation in the South under the leadership of Ngo Dinh Diem. The United States also began to structure the South Vietnamese armed forces into a carbon copy of its own military and prepared the country to fight a mid-intensity conventional war against an invasion from Communists in North Vietnam.

Diem faced enormous challenges in governing South Vietnam, not least because of the small cadres of Viet Minh left behind in the South, known as Viet Cong, still advocating for the adoption of Communism in the country. He also faced several other civil insurrections of groups opposed to his rule. Charges of corruption also plagued his government. Despite sometimes-tense relations with the United States, he managed to retain U.S. support for his shaky regime. Then, in 1956, he announced that the Geneva-mandated reunification elections would not be held, as he feared the Communists would win such a contest. Full-scale insurrection against Diem resurfaced in 1957.

The nature of the U.S. advisory role changed in the early 1960s. In December, 1960, the Communist government in North Vietnam announced the birth of the National Liberation Front (NLF) in South Vietnam, although the organization had already existed for at least a couple of years. President John F. Kennedy feared that Indochina was a prime theater for a Soviet takeover and he prepared to meet this global challenge. For the most part, however, Kennedy was optimistic. Like Secretary of Defense Robert McNamara and others of his advisers, Kennedy viewed Vietnam predominantly as a military problem to be "managed" successfully.

Background
World Leadership and Unclear Mission, cont.

Nevertheless, Kennedy and his advisers also had serious concerns about the political situation in Vietnam. U.S. leaders never persuaded Diem to undertake the reforms needed to win support for his government from the Vietnamese people nor to address seriously the corruption that engulfed the country. In his turn, Diem increasingly came to fear the escalating American presence as much as he feared his internal enemies. His concerns were not completely unwarranted.

As American journalists began to attack Diem and American's Vietnam policy, Kennedy became increasingly frustrated by Diem. Diem's heavy-handed and inept handling of a Buddhist uprising in the spring and summer of 1963 weakened American support for his regime. With his advisers greatly divided over what to do about Diem, Kennedy finally tacitly agreed to a coup effort by South Vietnamese generals against Diem in November, 1963, although Kennedy was shocked by Diem's murder during the coup. When Kennedy was assassinated three weeks later, Vice President Lyndon B. Johnson inherited a growing political and military quagmire.

President Johnson retained the basic policies of the Kennedy Administration. After an extensive policy review in March, 1964, the president concluded that "the only reasonable alternative" was "to do more of the same and do it more efficiently." Johnson expanded the number of advisers sent to South Vietnam and increased financial assistance to the nation. He hoped to keep Vietnam on the back burner at least through the 1964 presidential election, and he proceeded cautiously. However, at the same time, he authorized secret plans for possible military action against North Vietnam as punishment for supporting the insurgents in South Vietnam.

Meanwhile, political intrigue and instability dominated the South Vietnamese government as the civil strife escalated. The Viet Cong controlled more than forty percent of the territory and more than fifty percent of the population. In many areas, the Viet Cong were so entrenched that only massive military force would dislodge them.

On August 2, 1964, the budding crises between the United States and North Vietnam intensified with a North Vietnamese attack on the USS *Maddox,* which was engaged in electronic espionage in the Gulf of Tonkin off the North Vietnamese coast. The United States launched air strikes against North Vietnam, and Johnson seized the moment to extort from the frenzied U.S. Congress the Tonkin Gulf Resolution, which authorized the president to employ military power against Communist North Vietnam. Surprisingly, though, Johnson reverted to a cautious strategy after the Tonkin Gulf incidents, at least for the moment.

In 1965, the United States made the fateful decision to commit major ground combat forces to the war in Vietnam. On July 28, Johnson announced that he was sending more troops and that draft calls would be increased. The buildup of American troops moved into high gear. At the end of 1964, about 23,500 Americans were serving in Vietnam, but by the close of 1968, that number would grow to 525,000 with a steady stream of additional deployments.

Background
World Leadership and Unclear Mission, cont.

Beginning in early March, 1965, Johnson authorized a series of retaliatory air strikes against the North Vietnamese that continued nearly
unabated until October 31, 1968. It was in the conduct of the air war
that the greatest controversy arose over the administration's "graduated
response" approach. The joint chiefs of staff, as well as the field
command, sought to apply massive force in the shortest possible time.
Instead, frustrating impediments to this strategy were imposed by the
civilian hierarchy. Even though the scope and magnitude of the air war
continued to increase, the incremental pace permitted the Communists
to make adjustments and to put in place an air defense system. Johnson
eliminated the air strike program altogether in early November, 1968.

In June, 1964, General William C. Westmoreland took command of U.S.
land forces in Vietnam, devising a strategy of attrition and employing
search-and-destroy tactics. The measure of merit under this approach
became the body count; the objective was to reach a point at which
enemy soldiers were being killed at a greater rate than they could be
replaced by infiltration from North Vietnam or by recruitment in South
Vietnam. With a force of just over half-a-million men, Westmoreland
mounted large operations. The first of these engagements took place in
the Ia Drang Valley in November, 1965. When it was over, the
Americans had inflicted an estimated 3,561 deaths on the
Communists, losing 305 of their own in the process.

The American military establishment in South Vietnam grew larger with each passing year. An elaborate system of base camps was developed and ports and airfields were built or improved. Naval and air force elements grew proportionately, putting massive firepower at the military's disposal. But the Viet Cong infrastructure in the hamlets and villages continued essentially undisturbed. Nevertheless, U.S. military leaders sent fairly optimistic accounts of the progress of war back to politicians in the United States.

In January, 1968, the Viet Cong launched the massive surprise attack that became known as the Tet Offensive. The largest single battle of the war, the Tet Offensive saw the Communists attack five of South Vietnam's six major cities, as well as hundreds of smaller towns and villages. Although surprised by the attack, U.S. and South Vietnamese forces rallied against the offensive quickly and managed to push back the Communist surge within a matter of weeks.

After the Tet Offensive, however, General Westmoreland informed his superiors that he would need nearly 200,000 additional American troops to defeat the Viet Cong in South Vietnam, a request that surprised U.S. officials. Westmoreland had been describing the Tet Offensive as a battlefield victory, one that had cost the Communists severe losses. Now this request for hundreds of thousands more troops seemed to undermine the credibility of that claim, just as the fact of the Tet Offensive itself had undermined Westmoreland's optimistic forecasts for the progress of the war.

Background
World Leadership and Unclear Mission, cont.

His request precipitated a review of American policy on Vietnam. The result was a series of dramatic changes, all with the goal of capping U.S. involvement and shifting the main burden to larger and more capable South Vietnamese forces. The high-water mark of American commitment to the war had passed. Westmoreland himself was replaced as U.S. commander in Vietnam by General Creighton Abrams on June 11, 1968.

Abrams changed the tactics from "search and destroy" to "clear and hold," changing the measure of success from body count to population security, and the philosophy to conducting "one war" in which pacification, improvement, and the conduct of military operations were all integrated and of equal importance. Abrams understood the war and the influence of the home front support base, and he understood the need to work within the limits of that waning support. For a number of years, public, congressional, and, to some extent, even media backing had been strong, but that had been lost as year after year went by with no discernible progress in bringing the war to a successful conclusion. American protests against the war on the home front, particularly on college campuses around the country, were becoming louder and gaining ground with every month that the war dragged on.

With the advent of the Nixon administration in Washington in early 1969 came formalization of a drastically changed approach to the war in Vietnam. "Vietnamization," the process of progressively turning the burden of fighting the war back over to the South Vietnamese as American forces disengaged, became the dominant theme. Beginning in August, 1969, the U.S. government began withdrawing American ground forces from Vietnam, beginning a steady stream of troop reductions that was nearly complete by the spring of 1972. At the same time, the revised tactics specified by Abrams involved remaining American combat units in thousands of small patrols by day and ambushes by night.

In the spring of 1970, President Nixon authorized U.S. forces to do something about Communist bases in Cambodia and Laos. Launching attacks coordinated with the South Vietnamese, American forces drove into Cambodia on a sixty-day rampage that captured thousands of tons of weapons and ammunition, supplies of every description, and piles of documents. A major benefit of the Cambodian incursion was the choking-off of the Communists' lifeline of supplies. The operation was believed to have bought up to a year's additional time for Vietnamization to progress, as well as providing increased security for the dwindling American forces.

In late January, 1971, there followed another attempt to sweep enemy sanctuaries and disrupt the major supply line from North to South Vietnam along the Ho Chi Minh Trail. This effort consisted of a large-scale raid by South Vietnamese forces into southern Laos. U.S. forces had by this time been prohibited by Congress from engaging in ground operations in Laos or Cambodia, so they played a supporting role in the operation. Again, many supplies were captured or destroyed, and the Communists took horrifying casualties, but the results were mixed. South Vietnamese units had been operating for the first time without their American advisers, an arrangement that proved problematic when it came to calling for various kinds of assistance, from artillery to medevac to close air support. Meanwhile, the Communists, relieved of any necessity to leave forces to defend the North by the perception

Background
World Leadership and Unclear Mission, cont.

that U.S. policy prevented ground intervention there, were able to concentrate virtually their entire military establishment in the path of the invading forces. Nevertheless, severe losses had been imposed on the Communists, and additional time was gained for Vietnamization to proceed.

One measure of the effectiveness of the cross-border operations into Cambodia and Laos was that it took the Communists until the spring of 1972 to gear up for another major offensive. When it came, however, it provided a severe test of the expanded and improved South Vietnamese armed forces, now left with only air, naval, and logistical support from the Americans. In what came to be known as the Easter Offensive, at the end of March, Communist forces struck in force at three key locations—along the Demilitarized Zone, north of Saigon around An Loc, and in the Central Highlands at Kontum.

These attacks triggered major retaliatory strikes by U.S. air and naval forces, including renewed bombing of Hanoi and Hai Phong in North Vietnam for the first time since the halt ordered by Johnson in November, 1968. Large numbers of additional ships and aircraft were dispatched to the theater of war, and Hai Phong and North Vietnam's other major ports were mined, an action often urged by military leaders but never before authorized by civilian authorities.

The South Vietnamese fought well, and Abrams asserted that they had made great progress over the past year, although American support remained crucially important. In late June, 1972, Abrams departed Vietnam after five years of service there and headed home to be army chief of staff. He was succeeded as commander by General Frederick

Weyand, his deputy for the previous two years and a man with vast
experience in the war. Weyand inherited the difficult and thankless task
of closing down the American expeditionary force.

Apparent progress in the Paris peace talks had hit a snag in late
autumn of 1972, and although Secretary of State Henry Kissinger had
reported virtually on the eve of the U.S. presidential election that
"peace is at hand," the prospect seemed to fade away. Ever-narrowing
U.S. expectations and aspirations for the war now focused on the
return of American prisoners of war. On December 18, Nixon unleashed
the most concentrated bombing campaign of the war on North
Vietnam. The onslaught continued until December 31, when the North
Vietnamese agreed to resume the peace talks. Agreement was then
swiftly reached, and on January 23, 1973, the document was initialed
by Kissinger and Le Duc Tho. The Paris Peace Accord (1973) called for a
cease-fire, the withdrawal of all U.S. military forces within sixty days,
the return of all captured personnel, efforts to locate missing persons
on both sides, and the beginning of talks aimed at achieving "national
conciliation and concord."

Although U.S. involvement in Vietnam steadily diminished after the
signing of the Paris Peace Accords in 1973, it did not cease altogether.
Immediately after the Paris agreement, a number of U.S. bases were
signed over to the South Vietnamese and enough planes and helicopters were brought in to give the South Vietnamese the fourth largest
air force in the world. At least 9,000 U.S. servicemen hastily resigned
their commissions so that they could be legally retained by the
Vietnamese as civilians. President Nixon also ordered occasional reconnaissance flights over North Vietnam so that he could match his

Background
World Leadership and Unclear Mission, cont.

previous promises to supply $4.75 billion in reconstruction aid with threats to drop the aid and resume bombing if the cease-fire failed to hold. The U.S. Air Force also continued to bomb both Cambodia and Laos during this period.

Deeply upset by the disclosure of illegal bombings in Cambodia, on May 10, 1973, a rebellious, heavily Democratic Congress cut off all funding for further U.S. air operations in the theater. By late June, Congress went further to pass a law forbidding further military operations of any sort in Southeast Asia. Nixon's angry veto was overridden after negotiations extended the final deadline to August 15, 1973. By November 6, 1973, Congress overrode another Nixon veto, and the War Powers Act became law, requiring the president to inform Congress within forty-eight hours of the dispatch of U.S. troops to another country and specifying that the troops must be withdrawn within sixty days unless Congress explicitly authorized their presence.

Meanwhile, Nixon began to experience political trouble at home on a number of issues, including the emerging Watergate scandal. The decline in his political power, combined with increasing war weariness among Americans, undercut his military efforts in Southeast Asia. Despite intense Nixon administration lobbying, Congress cut the amount of aid authorized for Vietnam dramatically in 1974.

In August, 1974, after the Watergate scandal forced Nixon to resign from office and Gerald Ford assumed the presidency, American interest in Vietnam declined even further. Secretary of State Kissinger still talked of preserving American credibility in the region and lobbied hard for continued aid, but a generally hostile Congress cut appropriations for

1975. Even charges that Americans might still be held against their will in Vietnam were largely discounted by a war-weary public.

The decline in American interest in Vietnam became clear to the world when the United States did not respond to the North Vietnamese push far into South Vietnam during the first half of 1975. The South Vietnamese government surrendered on April 30, 1975, a mere fifty-five days after the final Communist offensive began. As television screens in America displayed dramatic images of Americans being evacuated by helicopter from the roof of the U.S. Embassy in Saigon, Communist forces quickly solidified their power in Cambodia and Laos as well.

After the fall of the South Vietnamese government in April, 1975, the United States conducted a punitive policy toward Vietnam. The U.S. government refused to normalize relations with the newly reunited state and actively sought to isolate Vietnam politically, economically, and diplomatically. The two countries did not establish normal diplomatic relations until July, 1995.

Background
Casualty and Troop Strength Figures for the Vietnam War
World Leadership and Unclear Mission, cont.

Year	Strength
1960	800
1961	2,100
1962	7,900
1963	10,100
1964	14,700
1965	116,800
1966	239,400
1967	319,500
1968	359,800
1969	338,300
1970	254,800
1971	141,200
1972	16,100

Source: Tucker, Spencer C., ed.
Encyclopedia of the Vietnam War, 1998

Casualty Type	Army	Air Force	Marines	Navy	Total
Killed in Action	27,047	1,080	11,501	1,306	40,934
Died of Wounds	3,604	51	1,482	152	5,289
Missing in Action, Declared Dead	261	589	98	137	1,085
Captured, Declared Dead	45	25	10	36	116
Missing, Presumed Dead	118	0	3	2	123
Other Deaths	7,143	841	1,746	932	10,662
Total*	38,218	2,586	14,840	2,565	58,209

*This figure includes casualties recorded from November 1, 1955 to May 15, 1975.
Source: Department of Defense Personnel and Procurement Statistics.

Country	Military Dead	Civilian Dead
United States	59,000	–
Australia and New Zealand	475	–
Thailand	350	–
South Korea	4,407	–
North Vietnam (including Viet Cong)	1,000,000	100,000
South Vietnam	225,000	300,000

Source: Bowman, John S., ed, Facts about the American Wars, 1998.

Additional Resources

- Using This Resource Book

- Integration into National History Day

- Using ABC-CLIO Websites for Researching Nation-Building

- Additional Nation-Building Topic Ideas

Using This Resource Book

The *Triumph & Tragedy* resource books are designed to provide teachers with all the materials to create interactive lessons centered on a single important topic of American history. In each lesson, the students are asked to analyze primary historical documents and draw conclusions about the topic. You will find two sets of suggested classroom activities in each resource book. For each activity, we have provided background essays, source documents, and reference pieces.

The materials are organized as follows:

1. INTRODUCTION

The essay in this section is a broad overview of the resource book's topic. You may use it to create a general lesson or lecture on the issue at hand, or to prepare students for the historical analysis portions.

2. THROUGHOUT HISTORY

The material provided here is geared to a specific sub-topic within the broader issue; for example, the role of work in immigration or the legal aspects of free speech. This material may be used to create a preparatory lecture for the resource book's interactive portions, or copied and handed out for the students to read.

3A & 3B. DEFINING MOMENTS

Two key historical events are presented in each resource book that illustrate the problems and complex forces at work within each issue. The Defining Moment sections begin with short historical background essays that contextualize the historical event. Again, these pieces may be used to organize a short presentation or given to students to read before beginning the activities.

4A & 4B. CLASSROOM ACTIVITY

Each Defining Moment has a Classroom Activity attached. The Activity is broken down into parts, with materials required for each part of the Activity noted. When the Activity calls for Activity Sheets, these are located with the Activity description. In some cases, each portion of the Activity may stand alone, but they are designed to be cumulative. The last part draws on the lessons of the earlier parts, making it the most comprehensive. Some lessons are designed to take up a full class period, some are shorter, and some require homework assignments. The teacher will need to determine what is appropriate for his or her class based upon allotted time and teaching goals.

5A & 5B. PRIMARY SOURCES

The historical documents, images, cartoons, etc. called for in the Classroom Activities are in this section, each piece designed to be reproduced for the students. At the end of the Primary Sources are reference sources: glossary words, information on important laws, difficult quotes, background essays, etc. The teacher may wish to make handouts or overheads of this material, or write some of the information on the board to help the students with unfamiliar vocabulary or concepts.

We hope you find this format user-friendly and that you are able to adapt it easily to your students' needs.

Integration into National History Day

The theme *Triumph & Tragedy in History* is an excellent backdrop for historical research surrounding issues of nation-building. As the stories of different approaches of nation-building were presented in this workbook, the complexities and risks of failure became clear. The tensions between internal and external nation-building invite historical research.

The issues surrounding nation-building are complex, compelling, and relevant; all are excellent qualities of a National History Day research project.

National History Day engages students in historical research. After selecting a topic related to the NHD annual theme, students conduct research into primary and secondary sources. They enter their final projects in competitions using one of four different presentation formats: paper, performance, exhibit, or documentary.

National History Day projects ask students to determine the historical significance of their chosen topics. Projects related to nation-building can be approached using different research processes:

- Using primary and secondary documents to place the topic into historical perspective
- Building a timeline of events leading to the conflict to illustrate the significance of the topic
- Presenting an analysis of the conflict through the introduction of the historical context and people involved to deepen historical understanding

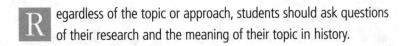

R egardless of the topic or approach, students should ask questions of their research and the meaning of their topic in history.

1. Who were the people involved?

2. What were their motivations?

3. Why did the incident occur at this time in history?

4. What was gained and what price was paid?

5. What were the long term effects of the court case?

Happy researching!

Complete guidelines and more information can be accessed at

WWW.NHD.ORG

Using ABC-CLIO Websites for Researching Nation-Building

The ABC-CLIO Schools Social Studies Subscription websites combine reference material, curriculum, current events, and primary sources in a single resource to help make historical research straightforward, accessible, and exciting for students. They provide students with the tools they need to investigate and assess the important questions associated with the topic of nation-building. Questions to consider include:

What is nation-building? Has it been successful? Why or why not?

What are the motivations behind nation-building?

What are the difficulties associated with nation-building?

How have different societies over time viewed nation-building?

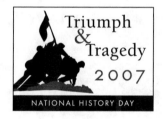

With these websites, students can find entries related to the topic of nation-building that link to related reference and primary source material, providing historical context that will help students develop their skills of source evaluation and historical analysis. Teachers can construct customized research lists of reference entries, images, maps, and documents, enabling students to compare, contrast, and analyze a variety of related resources.

ABC-CLIO's social studies subscription websites:

- Provide students access to deeper and broader content than other social studies resources, allowing students to synthesize what they learn from reference material and primary sources
- Combine reference, curriculum, and current events, which are updated daily
- Are correlated to curriculum standards, key assessments, and major textbooks
- Meet the needs of students for different grade levels and assignments
- Provide access from school and home for students and faculty

Additional Nation-Building Topic Ideas

1. The Treaty of Versailles: Self determination gone wrong

2. Justifying Rebellion: John Locke and the right to revolution

3. Simon Bolivar and Latin American Revolution

4. The Boxer Rebellion: China's fight against foreign power

5. Jose Marti and Cuba's War of Independence

6. William Wallace and the Fight for Scotland

7. Nasser and Pan-Arab Nationalism

8. Carving out their Own: The creation of the state of Israel

9. Castro: The maximum leader of the cuban revolution

10. From Slave Uprising to Sovereign Nation: Haiti's war for independence

11. Pancho Villa and the Mexican Revolution

12. George C. Marshall and his Plan: Triumph and Tragedy in Western Europe

13. The American Revolution: Creating a new nation

14. A Wall Crumbles and an Empire Falls: The decline of the Soviet Union

15. Blood Diamonds: Sierra Leone and the fight for a nation

16. Falling Apart: The break-up of Yugoslavia

17. Breaking Apart and Coming Together: Germany after 1945

18. Forced Together and Coming Apart: From the Soviet Union to nation states

19. From Persia to Iran: Fanaticism builds a new nation

20. The Struggle for Ireland: Nationalism v. religious conflict